Freedom Farm

Center Point
Large Print

**This Large Print Book carries the
Seal of Approval of N.A.V.H.**

Freedom Farm

Jennifer Neves

CENTER POINT LARGE PRINT
THORNDIKE, MAINE

This Center Point Large Print edition
is published in the year 2021 by arrangement with
North Country Press.

The text of this Large Print edition is unabridged.
In other aspects, this book may vary
from the original edition.
Printed in the United States of America
on permanent paper.
Set in 16-point Times New Roman type.

ISBN: 978-1-63808-001-5

The Library of Congress has cataloged this record
under Library of Congress Control Number: 2021936921

Table of Contents

PART ONE
FREEDOM, MAINE
1976–1999

PART TWO
PALERMO, MAINE
2015–2019

Acknowledgments

This book would not have been possible without the incredibly generous, sincere, and honest guidance of Rebecca McClanahan, Brenda Miller, and Dinah Lenney. When I fought to proceed in the direction of slapstick comedy, they encouraged me to dig deeper and take the time to get to know myself. For this, I am forever in debt. A thank you also to the Rainier Writing Workshop MFA program for introducing me to a group of writers hell-bent on lifting one another up as we each find our own paths. A heartfelt thank you to my editor, Chelsey Clammer, for her good judgment, patience, and time. I am so grateful to have had her guidance and experience on this journey.

My deepest love and appreciation goes to my parents Tony and Helene Neves, for whom the Freedom Farm is a most personal exploration. Many of their stories became my stories, and so the credit for this collection should truly be shared. And for their parts in helping to collect the memories that served as inspiration for many of the essays within these pages, as well as their camaraderie through the years, thank you to Jason Neves, Luis Neves, and Matthew Neves.

Thank you also to Jaikari Rada (a.k.a. Ally) for

taking such wonderful care of my small people, and giving me a most precious gift: time to write.

And last, but certainly not least, thank you to my husband Nathan, and my energetic children for their willingness to come with me no matter what, even when my plans are poorly thought out and disaster is imminent. I can't think of any better traveling companions in this life.

Freedom Farm

Introduction

When I began this project, I imagined myself setting out to capture the essence of my early life, the bones of family lore, and the values that shaped who I am and who I will ultimately become. As I wrote, some stories moved easily from start to finish. There was a path and events traveled upon it as though they were blind to the possibility of anything else. Then, there were some stories that seemed to grind as stones caught in a gear, that turned on themselves, tangled, and frustrated. Through this process, I have come to understand that to appreciate the fullness of any one person's journey is to acknowledge there is no one story to describe it. In fact, there is no number of stories that do us humans justice. We are infinitely complicated creatures, connected to our own stories, but also to the places where our stories intersect with others—family, friends, and even strangers. It's easy to lose patience with this mess, to give up believing that, in the end, the stories we tell and retell might bring us closer to knowing our true selves. But maybe this idea of seeking resolution in any form is too tidy, and more important, too little to ask of *good* stories.

As a writer, I am hoping to go beyond the surface, to work toward the impossible goal of capturing the whole of something—myself. So I will keep writing. There are years of stories still untold, both behind and in front of me. It is also my hope that this exercise in self-exploration will at the very least entertain, and possibly convince readers that, for a short time, my stories are good company in their own complicated journeys.

PART ONE

FREEDOM, MAINE
1976-1999

The Freedom Farm.

Spilled Milk

It seems my father was born with a personality that has just now begun, some seventy years later, to fit him. To hear him speak of childhood misdeeds is to enter a strange world where morality, justice, and equality guide the behavior of an overt juvenile delinquent. In his recollection, he was a child who felt obligated to punish abuses of power, who took special offense to prejudiced teachers and institutions, and who, despite his outward appearance as a subversive, was actually a force for good.

I have in my mind a version of the incident that inspired his very first institutional insurrection. I cannot promise the details are perfectly recollected, or for that matter, retold, but isn't that the way with stories?

The catalyst was a small-minded teacher, a woman who belittled my father's Portuguese accent and poor circumstances. Was it the mispronunciation of a word that made her flinch? A word my father should have known but didn't, because he had just begun absorbing the English language? As if to prove the inferiority of her immigrant student, she assigned young Anthony the responsibility of carrying his classmates' milk bottles, which I imagine as hunks of fluted glass, hazy and imperfect. Each morning Anthony was to fetch the wooden crate that carried twenty-four half-pint bottles from the school's basement kitchen and carry it to a third-floor classroom.

Being punished for a non-crime was a policy that did not sit well with my precociously fair-minded father. Ignorance is different than stupidity, he would always say, gearing up to tell his favorite part of the story. As he remembers it, on the first day he carried the rack of milk bottles up four flights, anger tightening his chest, a powerless player in a grown-up world. On the second day his feet fell like hammers, each step louder than the next—an outward expression of a deeply unsettling inner noise.

On the third day, my father climbed the stair-case slowly, with a tranquil expression his teacher might have mistaken for resignation had she stepped from the classroom to watch his daily penance. When he reached the third floor he leaned over the wooden ballister railing with the crate of glass bottles and, I'd like to think, took a moment to enjoy the silence. The boy in my mind would have relished the tingle of potential energy, would have appreciated the movement of his own digits as they opened, all at once straightening, gracefully releasing his burden into the open-air stairwell.

If the story is interrupted here, if the reader dwells even for the briefest moment on the question of young Anthony's *temper,* this thinking must be dispelled. A temper insinuates irrationality, does it not? A temper, by its very nature, cannot be trusted. Temper lacks control, lacks vision, lacks the sophisticated social maneuvering required to make a *point.* So let us continue.

He would have stayed to watch as the bottles gathered speed, shifting as the crate's imbalanced weight caused the metal grid's hold on the bottles to tilt and the contents to slide. He would have stayed to hear the shattering, to hear the crate bounce upward just after impact and to see milk explode into a million droplets. A smile would likely have appeared, for the briefest moment, at the corners of his lips before he returned to the class to report the "accident."

I'm certain young Anthony was punished for dropping the milk bottles, but he doesn't remember that part of the story, or if he does, he doesn't tell it. He remembers being relieved of his duties forever. He remembers a victory.

Like many of my father's stories, this one has the texture of a well-constructed fable, driven by an undercurrent of vigilante justice, and a message of empowerment.

A colleague recently asked me to think of the three stories I tell about myself, the three stories that pop to mind in awkward social settings that beg for a good personal narrative to break the ice. Although I haven't yet compiled that list, the question has since been lodged in the back of my mind, waiting, asking. What do our stories say about us? Why do we choose the stories we tell? Why do we repeat the stories that are told to us?

My father had a way of recounting his youthful indiscretions, molding each malefaction so that every retaliative act, violent outburst, or example of disorderly conduct could be traced neatly back to Quixotic benevolence in the pursuit of liberty and justice for all. Like the mathematician he would later become, he could not walk away from an ethical equation out of balance. The personal cost of surrendering was far greater than any disciplinary action he might face for not surrendering. Where did this value system come from?

When I was fourteen or fifteen years old, I had a soccer coach who scared some girls so much they'd run until they convulsed with pain, vomit pouring from their mouths, or they'd pass out from exhaustion. These were smart girls, strong girls, but also girls who would rather be unconscious than face Coach's wrath and disappointment. The man was intense. His muscles were always clenched, ready to sprint out onto the field to demonstrate an overlapping run, or the roughness with which he expected us to protect the ball. His eyes were fierce, a blue or green is what comes to mind, but in truth it wasn't the color that made them so intimidating. His eyelids, like the rest of his muscles, were tight, ready to explode upward, coiled in anticipation of the next shock. Coach's nose was straight if you looked him in the face, but in profile it bumped and dipped several times from bridge to tip, a nose roughed up by sports and, I'd always imagined, fists. The thing that made girls quake, turned their skin clammy and bloodless, was his voice, a low bellow, a glottal howl, eerily animalistic. It was angry, forceful, loud. With it he pulled the best from some, and others, maybe the smart ones, quit.

It would never have occurred to me to leave the team. I admired Coach. I relished the challenge. I chanted the words to Rudyard Kipling's *Law of the Jungle*. I chanted "Break Bones!" I chanted whatever this maniacal man thought I should chant to bring forth my fiercest self. I was fast. Scored goals. I found my own howl.

Girls dropped like flies from the squad. Eighteen, seventeen, sixteen, and as we neared the number of girls required to field a team at all, Coach's agitation bordered frenzy. Repeated incidents of regurgitation and heatstroke merely confirmed his team's lack of preparation. Dizzy spells and forehead bruising were signs of progress. He could not fathom why girls were quitting. He was infuriated by their cowardice and irked that we, those who remained, could not convince the deserters to stay. Why couldn't we make them understand that enduring was to triumph over their own weakness?

Then, Emily quit. As Captain, I had been trying for weeks to convince Emily that it would get better, that she was doing her best and we all loved her for how hard she worked. We wanted her on our team. She was our friend. Coach was just in a bad mood; he didn't hate her, or want to cause her permanent brain damage when he insisted she take punt after punt with her forehead. But Emily quit anyway.

I broke the news to Coach, knowing he'd be upset and hoping he'd see the need for a softening, a slight correction in the direction of kindness, maybe compassion.

He called out for the team to gather. Fourteen of us, our shin guards caked with mud, bodies slick with acrid pubescent sweat. We'd circled center field before he reached us, his gait calculated, his face like brown stone, still and cold. When he spoke, spittle collected at the corners of his thin lips, his thick legs were tense, muscles bulging from above the knee. I had never seen anyone so angry, so poised to strike. He accused us, swung his freckled arms violently toward our faces, as we stared wide-eyed back at him. "Emily quit because of you!" He screamed. "Point at yourselves."

The girls' faces went white, and when their

fingers didn't rise, Coach screamed again, "Point!" I watched, helpless as fingers rose to point directly at the chests of their owners. Coach continued spitting curses and deriving what looked like pleasure at this communal admission of guilt. Pointer fingers hung, as if creatures all their own, hovering, blaming the bodies that moved them—all but one.

My arms hung, relaxed, at my sides. I looked at my friends, young women belittled, bullied by this man, and I smiled.

Coach's face darkened. Did blood vessels pop in his cheeks as I grinned, or is that a detail my memory has created for dramatic effect? I can still see his face, glowing red hot, mostly angry but maybe a little shocked too. Shocked at the audacity, the irreverence.

"Neves." He growled. "Point at yourself."

"No."

Such a simple word. I think back and I wonder, where did it come from?

"What?" His lips pulled taught against clenched teeth causing a thin white line to appeared just outside of the pink, an outline, a delicate accentuation of his disbelief.

The girls all turned to look, jaws dropping. Was I a fool?

"No."

I can't remember if I explained further or not. I can't remember if I told Coach that he was crazy

21

to think it was our fault because we'd been trying so hard to keep Emily happy, trying so hard despite how hard he was on her and on all of us. I can't remember how practice ended that day, or how the season ended that year. I do remember that Emily never came back to the team and the next year Coach had moved on to another team.

This is my story and it isn't. I have thought of that day, that "no," a hundred times since it happened and every time I have wondered, who was that girl?

Is this the power of stories? Do they give rise to the instinct for self-preservation? What would have happened if I had raised a finger like the other girls, or if I had done nothing at all? And what would have happened to my father had he chosen a silent yes that day with the milk bottles?

I should be clear, I find it distasteful, inconsiderate really, when writers insist on including dream sequences in the middle of their essays and expect the reader to pay close attention, to glean meaning from the chaos of someone else's subconscious.

But I had this dream.

I am traveling in Costa Rica. In waking life I have never been to Costa Rica, so the reader would be justified in approaching this dream with a certain level of suspicion. *I have just arrived at a hotel in the middle of nowhere. I am alone and worried about finding a room when I happen across my father. His hair is dark, his beard full—even though he is a young man again, I recognize him and I can tell he recognizes me. But, the strangest thing . . . I haven't yet been born. We are the same age, staring at one another like . . . well, like family. I tell him "I am your daughter" and he accepts this, hugs me with genuine—what? Relief? Sadness? He is on his way to the airport and tells me so. We both acknowledge this is the last time we'll ever see one another, at least, like this.*

This is how I imagine our stories colliding, my father's and mine. On equal ground in some timeless place where people and their troubles are always coming and going. This is how I know my father. Our values mirrored in our experiences, in our choices, in our stories.

And then there is this: I learned visualization from that bellowing coach. Learned to watch myself kicking goals, making perfect crossing passes, heading the ball into the net. I spent hours playing soccer off the field. I played while eating dinner. I played in line in the cafeteria. I played during English class. Maybe all that visualization helped and maybe it didn't, but I took to it.

So when my father tells this story, it is me in the musty basement of his elementary school in Massachusetts. I am the one with a crate full of bottles, too heavy and too unjust. I am the one learning, each time the story is told, how to say no. Over and over again, I drop the bottles, watch them shatter, and feel victorious.

Priscilla

Priscilla the pig was long gone by the time I came around, but for a few good years my father held her in high regard. She may have been destined for a couple of roasts and some sausage, but it never occurred to her to squander what little time she had.

I'm getting ahead of myself.

I want to start at the beginning. But, where is that? Where does a family begin? A marriage? A birth? Was it in 1919 when my paternal grandfather, age four, snuck sips of moonshine in the stowage deck of an immigrant ship? He was tipsy when he and his mother disembarked at Ellis Island and, as the story goes, was lucky to make it through customs, as officials thought he might be suffering a nerve condition. Four-year-olds aren't known for their impulse control and though I've never seen it, I can only assume that drunken four-year-olds are considerably more challenging.

Was it in 1669 when my maternal ancestor, Charles Gingras, arrived in Quebec? Or maybe it was in 1675, when Charles married Francoise Amiot and collected her dowry of 500 livres. Was this a lot of money for Charles? Did he think the deal a good one? Was he in love?

These are questions for which I have no answer.

For a long time I was consumed with tracking the tendrils of our family tree, Portuguese immigrants from Madeira on my father's side, Canadian merchants, nuns, and doctors on my mother's, but the more I learned, the less it seemed to matter. These people are not family; they are relatives. Family is more like an organism, entangled symbionts moving together through time. My family, the family to which Priscilla belonged, started with the signing of a deed. It began in the town of Freedom, Maine, on a piece of land with old rock walls, a farmhouse, and a cemetery.

Priscilla the pig was not my parents' first animal, but there is tenderness in their voices when they speak of her. She was more than a pig. What more, I cannot say. I never met her, and in all honesty, the pigs I *have* met did not strike me as being particularly noteworthy. In any case, I record the story of Priscilla the pig in an attempt to preserve a memory that was in no way mine, but that became mine—became a burl in our family's branch of an ancestral tree—through the retelling.

Shortly after my parents moved to the Freedom Farm, Priscilla was tasked with clearing out and cleaning up the overgrown cemetery on the property. Pigs are quite skilled at rooting up and eating just about anything in their paths and Priscilla was no exception. Prior to her start date, my parents built a lovely rock wall around the area using stones pushed to the surface of their bean fields by spring frost heave. My father made quick work of installing a temporary electric fence, moved a water trough, and my mother lured Priscilla to the jobsite with a bucket of grain and a few kind words. The pig took to the task with an entrepreneurial spirit, dislodging tuberous blackberry roots, eating clods of rogue alfalfa, and discouraging unwanted apple seedlings.

Her good work did not go unnoticed.

For optimal cinematic effect, this next scene should take place late in the day: The sun is well on its way to the tips of the evergreens that line the rear of the property. My father is sitting atop the spring-mounted scoop seat on his rusted red Super C tractor. Its front tires are so close together they fit handily between two rows of beans. The quality of the afternoon light gives the tractor's metallic body, blistered and worn, the appearance of ancient skin. Through the sharp clatter of stones beneath his plow blades, my father hears the stannic pings of buckshot colliding with the corrugated tin roof of the machinery shed. My mother hears the shots too. The bullets are whizzing just over her crouched body as she weeds her vegetable garden.

Looking up from his work, my father notices

one of the Gunderson boys, bent at the waist, nervously glancing about as he trots from the front to the back of his singlewide trailer, clutching a shotgun. He'd been aiming at Priscilla.

It's strange to think of my parents as outsiders, but that's what they were back then. They were well-to-do white collars, making fools of themselves on a farm with too much land and not enough equipment. At least, this is what the Gundersons must have thought, watching my father toil over acres and acres of an unfamiliar crop. If I ever caught the name of the lone gunman in the Priscilla story, I don't remember it. It never seemed important to distinguish which Gunderson had pulled the trigger. I am ashamed at my own comfort with this kind of ambiguity while simultaneously certain that I am justified in blaming each and every one of them.

There were several trailers and one house on the Gunderson property for much of my childhood. I never knew who lived where or in what relation to the others, but my mother always knew. She kept track of Gunderson family news, passed romance novels purchased at lawn sales to one of the elderly matriarchs, and bought Tupperware from another when the season for selling it rolled around.

I remember sneaking off into the woods just before the Gunderson property when walking with my mother. I was terrified of getting dragged into a conversation with Polly, the Gunderson who'd suffered a stroke years before. My mother could understand her, but I couldn't. Polly's speech was badly slurred, but it was more than that. She had no teeth left to shape the vowels as they passed through her wrinkled lips. Her mouth moved and sound came out, but to me the words were unintelligible. I did my best to smile when cornered on her porch, holding tight to my mother's sleeve, but always left feeling lost and guilty. It was a guilt that lingered, tickled the corners of something I wasn't sure I wanted to understand.

But this story isn't about the Gundersons. It's a story about a pig.

As far as cemeteries go, ours was quite large considering the number of known occupants— two, if you counted Priscilla, there were two. Hannah Commings was the second, and though she'd been there substantially longer, it was difficult to determine who was more at home. As a child, I spent long hours imagining what fate Hannah had succumbed to. She died young. In my memory, the gravestone indicated early twenties, but in truth, I have not visited the cemetery in almost 25 years, so cannot be sure.

Although it might seem strange to designate the enclosure a cemetery, it never occurred to any of us to call it something different. The number of graves was irrelevant. It was the space that mattered, clearly set apart from the rest, meant for burials.

It was Hannah's memory my parents were trying to honor when they delegated the cleanup to Priscilla that summer. In its overgrown state, the cemetery had been long forgotten by the town and my parents believed the Commings girl deserved to be remembered. Although I don't disagree, I suspect the impetus for restoration had as much to do with a fealty to the land than to historical preservation. Hannah Commings was part of the land and land was family.

Two weeks after the attempted assault on Priscilla, my father received a phone call from the Deputy Sheriff who informed him that he was to remove the hog from the cemetery immediately. When pressed, the local official could give no law-based justification, and so, quite reasonably, the directive was ignored.

It took another two weeks for the Deputy Sheriff to check back in. Meanwhile, Priscilla continued rooting, turning the long stagnant soil to reveal fresh, dark earth where there had once been overgrowth and underbrush. The cemetery was looking better and better by the day. When the Deputy Sheriff called for the second time, his orders came with explanation. A formal complaint had been lodged with the Sheriff's department. It was rumored that the woman buried in the cemetery had died of diphtheria, and the concerned citizen who'd called, no doubt a Gunderson, was certain that Priscilla was on the brink of instigating an outbreak.

Although the fear of deadly outbreak was a possible reason for gunshots and a call to the local authorities, there were more effective ways of settling a neighborly dispute. It was clear the Gundersons harbored some hostility toward my parents, homesteaders with the audacity to show up thinking they could do it better than the locals who'd been doing it for generations. The thing was, they *were* doing it better. Not because they had money, or special training, or expensive equipment. What they had was ingenuity, stamina, and discipline: in short, a work ethic.

The threat of diphtheria didn't sound credible to my father but he was not one to neglect due diligence. A man familiar with his resources, he placed a single phone call, spoke briefly to the front desk at the State Department of Health and Human Services, and was quickly patched through to the state epidemiologist. As he remembers it, the conversation with the woman on the other end of the line went something like this:

"Hello, it is my understanding that if someone died two hundred years ago of diphtheria, there is absolutely no threat of diphtheria in that grave."

"You are absolutely correct."

And so, my father did nothing to discourage Priscilla, who was speedily revitalizing the once-forgotten hallowed ground. I can only imagine the Gundersons' collective outrage at her continued presence. Did my father think himself above the law? Was this irreverence, this threat to public safety, a misguided show of superiority?

I grew up believing that attached to our parcel of land was an inescapable family rivalry. That a famous Hatfield-McCoy dispute that began in 1878 over a hog seems too perfect a chestnut. The Gundersons trespassed, smashed our mailboxes, harassed us on the school bus, and tried to kill our pig. Our eighty-acre plot of land abutted the property of several other landowners, but none were as undeviatingly irksome as the Gundersons.

It was us against them, even if the only Gunderson I had legitimate reason to avoid was the youngest. He was a foul-smelling, chubby-cheeked bully of a Gunderson named Toby. He must have been three or four years my senior, yet hovered indefinitely in the eighth grade. Freedom did indeed have a plague, but it wasn't diphtheria. Toby lurked at the edges of our property, called me names at school, and my brothers and I knew well the sound of his tiny bullets piercing perfectly round holes in the leaves of bean plants as we completed our weeding. I hesitate suggesting Toby was an excellent shot, but considering the number of shootings and the fact that a bullet wound was never reported, it seems unlikely that he was a bad one. I willingly admit, twenty years later, that while Toby was wrong to shoot in our direction, he showed remarkable restraint by purposefully missing.

But this story isn't about the Gundersons. It's about our family's first heroine. A pig admired for her tenacity and work ethic, who kept her head down despite chaos and injustice all around. She was a pig without fear of reciprocity.

My father too was unfazed by his confrontations with the Gunderson men. He made no attempt to pacify or even address them directly, since that didn't appear to be their way. My mother was perhaps a touch more accommodating than the rest of us, working to keep peace with the Gunderson women-folk. Likely this was an attempt to encourage Gunderson mothers to keep closer tabs on their sons and husbands. In hindsight it's impossible to determine if her efforts were rewarded. Yes, things could have been worse—but to presume this was the result of a maternal intervention seems too bold a claim.

In the Priscilla story, the Gundersons are permanently vexed by our presence. The looks on their faces as they peer from the mud-covered windows of their beige singlewide are ones of disbelief, anger, and fear. How offensive it must have been to watch Priscilla trot jauntily from one end of the rock wall to the other, flipping mossy stones with her snout, grunting with the pleasure of a job well done. Even our hogs were ambitious.

The next time the phone rang in regard to Priscilla's activities, it was not the Deputy Sheriff; it was the County District Attorney. "Sir," he said to my father, "you have continually ignored the Sheriff's Department in refusing to remove a pig from a cemetery."

My father showed no sign of regret, easily replying "I have."

In imagining this conversation, I have to wonder whether my father was tempted to inform the D.A. of the size of this cemetery. Did the D.A. imagine hundreds of graves being callously disrupted by a disorderly hog? Did my father appreciate the disproportionate level of authority being wielded by local officials in response to a cemetery of one?

The D.A. continued, "Do you understand that state law prohibits the desecration of cemeteries?"

And though he probably assumed as much, my father offered, "I didn't know that."

"Well I'm telling you now that having a pig in a cemetery is an act of desecration, and you need to move it."

The two men ended their conversation cordially and the D.A. likely took a few minutes to pat himself on the back for such an expeditious resolution to a pesky rural problem. My father on the other hand, a man in whom the distance between thought and action is undetectable, located the definition of desecration in the State's Revised Statutes, and discovered precisely what state law dictated in regards to Priscilla's temporary position as groundskeeper.

Desecration, as defined by State Law, was any act that "violates the sensibilities of an ordinary person." My father considered himself an ordinary person, and Priscilla's efforts to restore an historic cemetery hadn't violated his sensibilities at all. He left her where she was.

After the D.A.'s call, the Deputy Sheriff patrolled our road for a few days, presumably too cowardly to confront my father face-to-face. And what must he have thought, watching this creature roll in the muddy filth of her trough spillover? Priscilla's carefree attitude, her lack of respect for authority, her blissful ignorance, these were all signs of a delinquent pet, a menace to the community. Mr. Deputy Sheriff, frequently referred to as Hippity Hop the Cartoon Cop by my father, now personally insulted, took it upon himself to report Priscilla's continued presence back to the D.A., and again the phone rang. This time, the D.A. informed my father that such willful disobedience meant he was liable for prosecution.

I can imagine my father's voice, the words

leaving his lips, "Now wait one minute Mr. District Attorney . . ." I can hear the cordiality, the eerily calm tone of a man determined to teach a lesson to one sorely mistaken, ill-prepared government official. My father has a way of respectfully disagreeing, a skill that for many years, I took for magic—a kind of bureaucratic bewitching. I understand now that the origin of my father's power is a willingness to expend energy—sometimes an extravagant quantity and sometimes an embarrassingly miniscule amount—to investigate any particular topic.

In a confident yet understated manner, my father recited the statute's definition of desecration, explained his standing as an ordinary person, and informed the D.A. that his sensibilities had in no way been violated by Priscilla's efforts. The confounded D.A. had no choice but to agree that the cemetery job was arguably within the limits of the law, and of no concern to public health.

I also consider myself an ordinary person and the idea of a pig working to revitalize the cemetery has never bothered me, but something else has. There is an undertone to this family lore. An otherness my mother worked hard to overcome, but never did. In the Priscilla story, my father never interacts with the Gundersons face-to-face. He never addresses their fears, or dignifies their actions with a direct response. He doesn't extend empathy toward ignorance.

But this story isn't about the Gundersons. It's about the beginnings of a family: two people, a pig, and a cemetery. It's about outsiders asserting themselves, standing up for what they believed, and pushing against their boundaries. It's about working hard and using knowledge to combat ignorance and having the courage to question authority. Certainly there are limitations to the power of a story. Even though I see gray where once there was black and white, I still love the Priscilla story. Despite its faults, it celebrates the values on which my family was founded.

I have always felt my father's actions were justified, amusing even, because the Gundersons were wrong to be afraid. They were wrong to shoot a gun in our direction. They were wrong to call the police instead of talking to my parents directly. But this justification isn't fair. Fear isn't wrong or right—it's fear; it simply exists. What would I have done in my father's place? Would I have walked over to the Gundersons' trailer to ask why shots had been fired? Would I have acknowledged their concerns?

Priscilla took a bullet shortly after the D.A. backed off. She didn't stand a chance, nose pressed to the soil, eyes scanning for signs of unwanted flora. Her exposed picnic hams wagged from this side to that, as if flaunting her indifference to the indigenous Gunderson clan.

Whoever it was that fired those final shots

managed to hit Priscilla's tender hindquarters. I'd like to think she managed to keep from flinching as the buckshot lodged just beneath her bristled hide. In any case, she wasn't about to give up a sweet root bulb for the sake of self-pity, so continued working until my father approached to assess her condition. I derive special pleasure in picturing the whole of the Gunderson family staring out at our stoic hog, who, having been shot in the line of duty, seemed doubly determined to finish the job she started.

I've never asked what became of Priscilla in the aftermath of the incident with the Gundersons. I don't really need to. Whether she stayed to farrow piglets or went straight to the butcher's block, it's certain she did what needed to be done. As for the Gundersons, well, they weren't going anywhere.

The cemetery was about as clean as it was going to get so my father removed the #4 buckshot, moved Priscilla back to her pen behind the barn, took down the electric fence, and went on with life on the farm.

The Bees and the Pinto

On the farm, there was never too little time to fit in a quick chore. Each of our fields, those with beans, corn, alfalfa, and potatoes, was separated by a windrow, a ten-foot thick row of trees and brush. These were the places the old rock walls used to sit, and sometimes still did, buried beneath the overgrowth. One year, Pa decided to clean up a section of one of the windrows on Easter morning. "Clean up" is the sort of casual phrase my father would use to make the task seem more reasonable. If he had informed my mother that he intended to use a blowtorch to incinerate a forty-foot section of bramble in the twenty minutes before leaving for church and a family gathering, she wouldn't have taken quite so kindly to the idea. It was no secret that my father's distaste for family gatherings was unparalleled. He would argue that he'd just seen these same relatives five months earlier.

"What could they possibly have to report in such little time?"

While we kids loved visiting cousins, we were also well aware that the moments prior to a scheduled departure rarely passed without incident. For our father, the words "family party" elicited immoderate ambition and insufficient caution. Just out of earshot of our mother, he nonchalantly suggested that we should quickly slip into our work clothes and grab some matches. Matthew, the youngest, and unskilled in the art of covert operations, made no attempt to hide from our mother his delight at the prospect of a good fire. For her part, my mother continued readying herself for the party, holding out hope that this time, things wouldn't spiral out of control.

Pa started up the tractor and let us ride behind him, our feet balanced on the back edge of the winch as he rolled to the spot needing work. Thick brush was knotted at the base of an old rock maple, looking like a rat's nest—something our neighbor had once said about my uncombed hair. Dry grass grew below the dead limbs, its yellowed stems looking stiff and thick, like cigarettes. Matthew begged to be the one to light it. Pa said we were just going to burn a few spots, thin things out a bit before church. He let Matthew do the honors.

It burned just how Pa said it would. The mess was gone and the rock maple looked stronger standing alone. Since we still had four minutes, Pa hooked the winch to a downed tree, one that was big enough to cut into firewood. The tractor bucked its approval as the chain drew tight, pulling the thick trunk like a splinter from beneath the brush. One of my older brothers dragged the tree back toward the house while my father lit the blowtorch to ignite the scrub. We all watched as the flames climbed higher, higher, then jumped. I looked quickly to my father's face.

He was thinking.

He turned to my two older brothers: *The Boys.*

"Run to the barn. Get rakes. Get shovels. And get a bucket of water." He looked at Matthew and I and said, "Go get Mum."

I don't remember, but it is likely that our mother was already on her way out the door. She had a sixth sense about our father's diversion tactics, especially when fire was involved. Though he'll never admit as much, I think he knew that she was always the one exhibiting the appropriate level of concern in tight situations. I wonder if he might have fallen in love with her for this very reason. He must have known that successful child-rearing would require at least one parent capable of experiencing fear in potentially life-threatening scenarios.

While our father battled the flames alone, The Boys gathered every tool we had, dragging half a dozen rakes and shovels toward the mayhem. Matthew and I arrived shortly thereafter, our mother in tow. The alfalfa field, dry from a winter's exposure, was glowing orange in too many places to count. The flames had jumped right out of the windrow and started to spread in waves. Smoke billowed up into our faces, our lungs burned, and our eyes sprouted tears. We pounded the breaking edge of the fire with our shovels, raked dirt to snuff its spread. My father splashed the tree line with water, hoping to protect the woods. We were frantic as flames surrounded us, the heat singeing the hairs on our arms and our faces.

When the fires were finally out, we stood, spread across three acres of open field, looking at each other, our clothes black from ash and soot, our faces flushed, or burned pink from the heat. The fight had lasted for almost an hour. We waited silently for five minutes, maybe ten, to make sure the fire was really out. We waited until Pa yelled, "Let's go."

We hurried to the house, put on our Easter clothes, and drove into town. I have no memory of the ride, but I wouldn't be surprised if we sat in silence the thirty minutes it took to reach my Aunt Jackie's house. There was an unspoken sense of accomplishment—an energy coursing through the six of us that hadn't been there before. I remember the feeling, the buzz of adrenaline that escorts a day well lived, a story worth re-telling. My father is the type of man who stacks these kind of days one atop the other, seemingly without intention. He lives ferociously, and I wonder if this is what drew my mother to him so long ago, and keeps her by his side.

That Easter we missed church, but made it just

in time for lunch with my mother's family. When we walked into the house, noses turned, aunts and uncles stared, confused. My father's eyebrows were gone, his forehead noticeably longer. The Boys and I had crispy yellow lashes. Matthew's face was covered in pink and gray splotches and Mum had Band-Aids on her fingers. We stood before my mother's family like criminals on trial—a paroled gang of arsonists come to dinner.

Every spring it was the same. We picked rocks. One of The Boys would start the tractor, lift its bucket a couple of inches off the ground, and point it in the right direction. Admittedly, engaging a motorized vehicle's engine, setting the throttle just above idle and jumping off is probably frowned upon in the owner's manual, but tractors can pretty much drive themselves. We'd walk back and forth, back and forth, the tractor, like an obedient pet, followed just behind, puffing black smoke and shedding red flakes of rust. As it crawled its way across the dark spring soil, we would scramble before it, as a family, collecting rocks thrust up from a winter's frost and tossing them into the front-end bucket loader. Every so often one of us would jump up to adjust the wheel, ensuring our roving receptacle remained on course. When the bucket shrugged low with the weight of our labor, Pa would ask one of The Boys to dump the rocks. They traded this duty, taking turns behind the wheel, pulling hydraulic levers, adjusting throttle, and then jerkily driving off to lighten the load.

It was a family habit to refer to Luis and Jason as "The Boys." It made sense to me. Collectively they were a powerful entity capable of making my life miserable. Calling them The Boys showed a certain level of respect without divulging which of the two was more feared or favored in any particular situation. Both adopted five years before I was born and opposite each other in every way, it seemed appropriate to acknowledge their sameness. The Boys were my brothers. Despite being rather moody overlords, our tenuous relationship proved useful in certain circumstances.

Luis was gregarious. He was the only teenage boy I ever knew who could not only get away with giggling like a little girl, but could get an entire bus of stone-faced soccer jocks laughing with him. He was silly, sentimental, and always in the process of falling in or out of love. His dark eyes, dark hair, and dark skin made him a highly coveted novelty to the girls in his class—a fact he used to his full advantage.

Jason was a photo negative of Luis—light skin and hair, uncommonly humble, thoughtful and observant. He was prone to sadness, self-imposed bouts of isolation and unpredictably aimed anger.

He was shy in a way that made us all hurt a little, which I suspect he found irritating.

The Boys didn't like work for its own sake. For them, picking rocks was a chore and nothing more. To their credit, this is probably the sanest approach to such a task. Rocks needed to be removed to protect the blades of our father's plow and to ensure straight rows when planting time arrived. It needed to be done, but required no level of pleasure in the doing.

I cannot say with certainty why Matthew and I liked doing it. At first, it may have been the novelty, but novelty doesn't explain why, fifteen years of rock removal later, we are both nostalgic for those spring afternoons of manual labor.

In my earliest memories, Matthew would

Pa setting fire to a windrow to clean things up.

45

Pulling rocks.

choose the smallest stones. I think he liked the sound of rocks clattering into the metal bucket, each a victory bell that made our heads vibrate. I chose the biggest rocks I could find, used my whole body to twist and roll, wedge and wiggle them to the surface. Often the ones I chose were too big for me to lift alone. Pa would jog up and say, "Nice one," and then, "I've got it from here." And off I would run, scanning the horizon for the next big one.

In later years, I still chose rocks too big for me to lift and Matthew had grown stronger than any of us. His dark hair had started to curl, like mine, and his chest had expanded to accommodate the boom of a grown man's voice. He was the one who would see me struggling, would jog up, dig his dirt-caked fingers beneath the edges of rough stone, and straighten his back to lift.

Mum always walked close to the bucket, gathering stones just before they disappeared beneath the giant wheels, or just after they'd slipped past one of us. She made a point of conserving her energy, refusing to run back and forth, or throw rocks from far away. Every so often she would jump to one side or the other, dodging wild throws and ricochets.

Eventually The Boys went off to college. Jason found his place in a philosophy program and Luis decided after his first year to join the military. Matthew and I were left to take up the slack, and though each of our chores should have been doubled, I don't remember a change. In fact, I don't remember much about the time after The Boys left and before I did. Four years passed with just Matthew and me living on the Freedom Farm with our parents, but it's difficult to recall any specific memories about that time.

Farm life is rhythmic and cyclical. Maintaining a timeline of memories in a childhood spent spinning circles is nearly impossible. Summers weeding, autumns harvesting, winters sorting beans, and springs picking rocks. When I remember the seasons, we are all there, the six of us working together. We take care of the land and the land takes care of us. We are always together.

Jenny and the boys sorting beans.

• • •

When honeybee hives get too crowded, usually in the spring, they swarm. Our bees lived in hives that were stacked neatly beside the giant pile of rocks not yet shaped into a wall. It was my father who worked with them. He liked honey on his biscuits, which I suppose was reason enough for him to take up beekeeping. It might sound ludicrous, going to the trouble of keeping your own bees for a little honey on Sunday mornings, but it never struck me as odd. I grew up believing that wanting something was never a good enough reason to have it. Anyone can want. The pleasure comes in being able to provide for yourself. I find my own conviction in this approach to life a remarkable accomplishment on the part of my parents. How they managed to convince me that pleasure is derived from work is a wonder. As a new parent myself, I am eager to discover the secret of passing this philosophy to the next generation.

I don't remember how old I was when our bees swarmed, but if I had to guess, I was not yet school-aged. It must have been a weekend, likely the middle of mud season, when the queen made her move. She and a good portion of her worker bees left the hive in search of some new real estate. While sending scouts to evaluate the surrounding area, the swarm clung to the bowed limb of a beech tree at the edge of our fields.

Pa called us all outside, insinuating a need for assistance, even though we were all too young. He wanted to collect the bees that had deserted his hive and give them a safe place to spend the summer. He wanted their honey.

The Boys helped carry the chainsaw and mesh mask while Pa drove the tractor, bucket raised high, to rest beneath the undulating cluster dangling above our heads. Matthew was too little to understand the risk, so got right up close. Mum asked, "Is this a good idea?"

Pa's grin was as big as I'd ever seen it as he stood in the bucket next to the swarm. I could barely hear him over the rumbling engine of our pet tractor, but I knew from the shape of his mouth that he'd asked if we were all ready. I thought I was ready, so I nodded up to him. He winked, pulled down the mesh of his bee mask to protect his face, and yanked the cord that brought his chainsaw to life. The Boys stepped back, pulling Matthew and I away from the action.

As the story goes, while my parents were visiting my father's parents in Massachusetts, a neighbor ran into my grandparents' yard and informed my father that a swarm of bees had formed on his grapevine. The opportunity to expand his apiary was just too much to resist. He grabbed a covered corrugated box and pair of scissors and hurried to the swarm. Bees are generally docile at swarming time and soon the mass of humming bees was boxed for the return trip to Maine. My mother was deathly afraid of bees, but agreed to the adventure, having been assured that the bees would remain calm in the trunk for the duration of the trip, especially after dark. It is unclear whether either of them sincerely believed this or not.

Shortly after loading the swarm into the trunk and setting out for home, the bees began finding their way from under the back seat into the cab of my parents' yellow Pinto. Bees landed in my mother's hair, crawled at the cuffs of her sleeves, tickled her neck, and found the exposed flesh at her ankles. She wanted out, but my father was driving and saw no option but to continue on the road. In the retelling, I empathize with the panic, anger and sense of betrayal my mother may have been feeling—the helplessness. Yet I also understand, on a practical level, that there was no other option but to continue driving.

The first cut made by the chainsaw was to remove the end of the branch, the portion farthest from the trunk, beyond the swarm. The vibration didn't go unnoticed by the bees, but only a few seemed irritated by the disruption, zipping anxious patrols in erratic orbits. Pa didn't waste any time. He moved his blade to the other side of the nest and severed the branch a second time, sending the section covered in bees into the bucket beside his feet. Frozen, I watched defenders of the swarm rise up. One giant monster, black then gray then black again, against the skyline, poised for revenge. Was Pa laughing? I thought I heard him chuckling as he swung down, hands gripping the bucket edge, to land gracefully before us. Then they came. The bees were everywhere, my mother's screams of panic muted by the lull of angry buzzing.

I don't remember who grabbed me, but it was one of The Boys. Fingers dug protectively into the soft flesh of my side, the ground tilted, and my feet left the rocky soil, dangling awkwardly. We moved faster than my mother. My brother kept me tucked beneath his arm as my father shouted for him to move faster. Someone else must have grabbed Matthew, because I didn't see him anymore. I watched my brother's feet, his short legs stretching, calves tight beneath the strain of my weight. My own breath caught with each step as the arm that gripped my middle fought fatigue by squeezing more urgently. We ran that way, along the rock wall, through the alfalfa field, past my mother's garden plot, and into the front yard where the hazelnut bushes were just beginning to flower. We ran until my father called out, "We're safe!"

I have retold the story about my mother in that car with bees crawling all over her a number of times. It elicits a strong reaction from most people, sometimes horror at the idea of being trapped in a confined space with bees, other times a concern for the apparent lack of empathy exhibited by my father. I have been questioned about the authenticity of my casual retellings. Is this story harmful in some way? Have I done myself a disservice by not examining its implications fully? Certainly, my father could have been more considerate, acknowledged my mother's fear. And my mother could have, at any time, stepped from that car and found her own way home.

Stories like this one are imperfect. They can

be confusing to someone looking too hard for meaning. There is no question each of my parents could have said and done things differently. But they didn't. They rode five hours, sitting side by side, enduring the discomfort together. Honeybees explored their bodies without restriction and, against all odds, did not sting either of them a single time. Both of my parents have told this story. They tell it with their own spins, of course, but neither shows sign of regret.

That day in the Pinto, my mother and father were present, focused. They were doing something most people would never do. My mother was terrified, but she stayed. My father could have taken the trip alone, but he wanted her there. I've wondered at the reason for this. Was it an audience he sought, a witness to his antics? Maybe in part, but I believe that even more so, my father wanted my mother to participate, to be a part of the story.

It's no wonder he wanted us there the day he cut down and hived the swarm. He wanted us all to remember the excitement, our communal relationship with nature, and the thrill of stepping away from ordinary. My mother must have wanted us there too, despite the risk, or maybe because of it.

Slumped in the grass, having outrun our pursuers, we kids lay on our backs, panting. Mum was on her knees, shaking her head, breathing hard. She looked straight into my father's eyes. We thought she was mad at first, and maybe she was, but then she started to laugh. We all did.

The Pelt and the Generator

There must have been other things, clothes, blankets, maybe shoes, in my brother's closet, with its sloped ceiling and mothball musk, but I can't recall a single one. In my memory that closet, whose faded pastel wallpaper was peeling to reveal an ancient layer of velvety brown parchment, contained only two objects, neither of them belonging to my brother: a fox pelt and a static generator. Why is it I remember only these? I wonder, is memory alive in some way, sifting, sorting, extracting meaning from image? This is how I have always imagined dreams, a subconscious organizational tool, a way to see and learn from patterns in our waking life. Maybe remembering is like dreaming. It seems possible. After all, a dream and a memory have similar quality in recollection, a knowing without seeing. And so, what is it I know about these objects, about their relationship to one another? Is it as simple as mother and father?

The fox pelt was hidden at the bottom of a dry-cleaning bag. It wasn't the animal's death that captivated me, or the length of the straw-orange body as it draped lifeless across my shoulders. It wasn't even the unnerving curve of a clip-sewn lip or the sinew thin legs, dangling, sleek fur oily with years of casual fondling. It wasn't the feel of limp limbs adorned with hollow paws like miniature pom-poms waving as I walked, though if I'm being truthful, it didn't hurt that I found these details both perverse and oddly alluring. It was the fact that the fox belonged to my mother that drew me again and again to its hiding place.

It belonged to my mother alone. Certainly many things belonged to my mother, clothes, jewelry, perfume—but this was a thing without utility, an object with meaning and a history I could not begin to know.

I was a rule follower, afraid of disappointing my parents with disobedience, yet despite the pelt's status as "off limits," I couldn't resist sneaking into that closet for clandestine games of dress up.

I called my mother recently, nostalgic with the memory of prancing back and forth before the bathroom mirror with that awful fox in one compromising position after another. She remembered the fox well, black beads popped into empty eye sockets, sharp white teeth pulled and replaced with metal ones for fastening the lacquered nose to a coat or hat. "I miss that fox," she mused. "I had to throw it out. It was falling apart."

The pelt's demise was likely connected to excessive handling, and so I delivered a confession in the form of a question, confident that time had absolved me of any wrongdoing. "Did you know that I used to sneak into the closet to play with it?"

"No," my mother said with a laugh. Though, the length of the pause between question and answer seemed to betray a detour in her attention, a straying toward her own memory of this object. I didn't push the issue. Instead I asked, "Where did you get it?"

I had always assumed that a man other than my father had given the carcass as a gift, a poor judge of my mother's taste. Yet she'd kept it, unworn, tucked in a plastic bag in a closet I wasn't supposed to play in. A macabre token of a secret past.

"It was my mother's."

She recounted her own childhood memory of the fox pelt, admitting that she too snuck into her mother's closet to admire it. While swaying before a bedroom mirror, she had wrapped the fox just as I had, around her body.

The second object in the closet, more straightforward in origin yet equally captivating, was tucked neatly within the corrugated flaps of a cardboard box held together with layers of tape, the oldest of which were curled and crusty. Inside, a Van de Graaff generator, its metallic sphere balanced atop a conical shaft, sat lifeless. This device was my father's and was used at his discretion. It served no functional purpose, though if asked, my father might have argued it was a tool for educating children about electricity. In truth, it was a device that collected static in a giant metallic bulb and to the delight of everyone involved, shocked the individual brave (or foolish) enough to touch it. It was impossible to predict when he would choose to drag it from that closet, and so, to avoid the torture of anticipation, I worked hard to forget its existence between uses.

The Van de Graaff generator, a relic of my father's high school science fair project, was the kind of toy that never lost its magic. Even my father, a man who could make you feel guilty for calling it a day after ten hours of hard labor, could not help lighting up at the prospect of an evening spent with this contraption.

The family would gather around our kitchen's linoleum countertop. Stools squawked as the boys and I dragged them close, eyes riveted on our father as he assembled the pieces. The meticulous preparations extended well past any reasonable timeline, creating in us a sense of confusion. Never did a game feel so much like punishment as we watched our father pause to buff a dusty plug prong or walk to the stove to start water boiling for a cup of tea. He felt our eyes on him, knew our attention was undivided, and so used these moments to impart small wisdoms, though I'm not sure I remember a single one.

When the Van de Graaff generator was finally ready, we held our breath, eyes wide, ears pointed toward the metallic globe, waiting to hear the familiar hum of a spinning belt and the crackle of static. Who would be the first to reach a finger close, to brave the fear of the electrostatic shock, which was always worse than the shock itself? I can't recall if I was ever first, or if I was ever too afraid to touch the globe at all.

Why has memory only kept these two things in that closet? What pattern has been pulled from the commonplace? And if memory mimics dream, maybe I should come at these objects differently. Maybe I should admit that there is one more thing that I remember about the closet with the sloped ceiling. I recall vividly a secret passage that led to my room on the other side of the stairs. It was small, protected by a brown slatted door that opened inward. Behind the door were the rough-cut boards of the house's framing and just enough space for a child to crawl or hide. I remember feeling relieved, comforted that I had a place to go should danger present itself and a way to reach my younger brother, who slept alone in the room with the closet.

The thing is, there was no secret passage.

At first, I assumed the memory had been planted when I was a child, a dream that felt real, so transformed into more. But I'm not so sure this is the case. How does one pinpoint the moment a false memory was planted? What if this passage is more recent? What if it serves some purpose I have not yet recognized?

To dwell seems dangerous. Just as a dream falls through fingers when pulled to the light, a memory changes, becomes more or less than it really was when touched too many times.

I know this memory is real: We turned off the light and linked hands, my three brothers and I extended across the kitchen. Our father, at the end of the line, gently wrapped his hand around the curve of our kitchen's fluorescent bulb. The dim glow of the living room lamp filtered in from the hall, just enough light to watch as my mother, at the other end of the chain, slowly reached her extended finger closer and closer. When the spark finally jumped she yelped with surprise and for an instant the fluorescent bulb popped to life. My father encouraged her to touch the generator again, but this time to hold her hand against the globe, letting the static electricity pulse through our bodies uninterrupted.

The Cost of a Turkey

As the story goes, it was the cackling of alarmed turkeys that woke my parents that night. My older brothers and I were sound asleep in our bedrooms when the squawking started, but like many of the stories told in our house, this one has become so familiar I can tell it from start to finish from multiple points of view.

My father's eyes bolted open and in one motion his bare feet were pushed into the cold leather interior of his steel-toed boots and he was moving. My mother swore she remembered him jumping through their bedroom window into the pen, but my father recalls leaving through the front door.

The turkey pen hugged the side of our farmhouse, running from the equipment shed all the way to the road, its metal mesh fence an unnecessary formality as far as the turkeys were concerned. They knew where their food came from, and so rested easy in their enclosure.

As I imagine the scene, even if he'd been standing still, it would have been impossible to distinguish between my father's pale flesh and the white of his briefs in the moonlight. To old man Gunderson and his two boys, the approaching figure must have looked like death itself, naked and enraged, a specter moving through the tall grass outside the pen with purpose. Vile threats exploded from my father, one after another.

Gunderson and his boys had released their mutt into the pen, hoping the kills would be quick and quiet so that they might have a few turkeys for themselves. The attack had been neither, and within seconds of the first distressed putts and cackles my father was there, threatening the intruders and their dog. Old man Gunderson, plagued by cataracts and poor night vision, tripped as he turned to run. His two teenage sons watched in frozen panic, as their father lay helpless, injured, begging for mercy.

"Please, please don't hurt me! My dog got loose. We was just trying to catch him. Please! I'm hurt. My ankle! I can't get up."

My mother's voice was begging too from her spot on the front lawn. Wrapped in a bathrobe, she watched as her husband disappeared and his temper emerged. I picture her screaming his name over and over, "Anthony! Anthony!" hoping to pull him back, to rein him in.

Was it her pleas, or the old man's, that stopped my father? Or was it all a show, the slow backward swing of his heavy boot as he pretended to take aim at the man lying before him? Maybe it doesn't matter what stopped him. In the end, my father didn't kick the old man, he kicked the old man's dog.

● ● ●

I'm embarrassed to admit the number of hours I have spent imagining and writing about why the Gundersons might have felt they were justified in stealing those turkeys. I've given the old man and his boys the benefit of the doubt in almost every conceivable way. I've wondered how hungry they were, and whether I might have tried to steal if I were as hungry as they might have been. I've tried to understand the implications of their socio-economic class, access to education, and ability to communicate effectively in a potentially threatening situation. I've asked myself how anyone can blame anyone else for bad behavior since it's impossible to know the circumstances of others.

I've let myself dwell on unanswerable questions—questions about a family I will never know. All of this to avoid asking another question: How could my father, a man I do know, have kicked that dog? A part of me understands his actions that night. That dog had to be stopped, even if it was only doing what dogs do. Was a turkey's life worth hurting an innocent dog? For me, the answer is no. For my father, it was yes, and for him, it was not a question of innocence, but rather of establishing a clear respect for our property and its boundaries. Bottom line, my father was angry. And this is the root of it, the difference between him and me. I am paralyzed by anger. It is my instinct to turn inward, to avoid reaction in the service of self-preservation. I report this fact with no judgment. Whether my father's anger was justified or proportionate is just as impossible for me to know as the mental state of the Gundersons prior to their trespassing.

After the Gunderson boys helped pull their father to his feet, mine found the two dead turkeys and walked them to the car, its headlights off, trunk open, engine still coughing. He dropped the turkeys into the trunk and slammed it shut. Turning to the old man, my father's voice fought through clenched teeth, "You'll pay for those."

Weeks went by, then months . . . or was it years? Old Man Gunderson never sent a check or slipped an envelope under the door.

Each fall, as the Maine heirloom beans died on their stalks, my parents began preparations for harvest. They didn't have a bean puller yet and my brothers and I were too small to be of much use, so my parents hired day laborers from around town. Friends and neighbors were paid by the row to pick and pile dried stalks for the combine to thrash.

My father didn't have many compliments for Maude, but he did respect her work ethic. She and old man Gunderson, her husband, lived in a dilapidated trailer at the top of the hill. Our families weren't on the best of terms, but money was money and Maude was willing to work.

At the end of each shift, sweaty and sore, workers would report to my father with their totals. He would tally, record, and then pay them for their labor. I don't know if it was her first day on the job or her last that season, but when Maude approached my father for her pay, he calculated her profits, wrote the total on a piece of paper, and showed it to her. When telling this part of the story, my father always chuckles, "Her day of hard labor just about covered the cost of those two turkeys as far as I saw it."

So instead of digging through the stack of tens, fives, and ones at his belt, he looked her in the eye sternly and said, "You tell your husband that you just paid for those turkeys."

And here again, I am torn. Was one turkey's life worth this added injustice: a woman forced to pay for the misdeed of others. Not just others. Men. It shouldn't matter to me that it was a woman paying for men and not the other way around, but it does. It matters because I do not believe Maude was an equal in her home. I do not believe she could have stopped these men even if she'd wanted to.

Did she know about old man Gunderson's plan? Was she possibly the one who came up with it? These are also unanswerable questions. Irrelevant ones. Maude didn't try to steal the turkeys. Her husband and her boys did. Yet this distinction has never mattered to my father, at least, I've never heard him express guilt or doubt about doing what he did. Maybe this is because the story was never meant to be pondered or pulled apart to investigate the missing elements, which one might argue include compassion, communication, and forgiveness. The turkey story was more like a blunt-force instrument meant to demonstrate the importance of holding others accountable.

I have always loved the story for its clean resolution and its emphasis on personal justice. And despite my equivocations, I know the Gunderson men were not justified in stealing. They were attempting to get something for nothing.

What would I have done in my father's place? I don't know. The only thing that's clear? My father and I do not agree on the cost of a turkey.

But maybe I'm coming at it the wrong way. It seems too neat, this idea of cost. How can I ask what I might have done in my father's place when the truth of it is this: I would never have left the safety of my home. I would have listened as my turkeys squawked and were torn apart, too scared to confront that coward and his sons. I love this story because it lets me imagine myself staring down at old man Gunderson. I can feel the hairs on my naked flesh standing on end, the smell of blood in my nostrils, the cool confidence of righteousness deciding my next move.

Weeds

It is only through examination of recent events that I have begun to unravel the origins of my peculiar relationship with agriculture. I'm ashamed to admit that for the last five years I have let entire crops of carrots, onions, lettuce, corn, potatoes, and broccoli rot in the ground, go to seed, and sour on the stalk. In truth, I don't even like broccoli. I plant it, but I have never once intended to harvest its foul bounty.

This level of produce negligence weighed heavily upon me until I discovered the underlying problem, for which there is no cure, and for which the only treatment is a yearly dose of vegetable sacrifice. Truth is, I am not a good gardener. Many people inexperienced in the art of food-growing, take up a spade and work the soil every day. They learn as they go, and usually their gardens provide a level of sustenance appropriately proportional to the effort expended in their upkeep. But my condition is not based on a lack of skill or confidence; it is a rare and private struggle having to do with an emotional apathy toward fruit-bearing vegetation. I don't really care about the vegetables. What I'm after is the satisfaction of taking control of an unruly garden. I garden to get rid of the weeds.

I might even go so far as to say: I was born to weed.

I am suspicious that my proclivity for the identification of invasive species was genetically orchestrated. My father: the farmer, the mathematician, the man with unparalleled focus and an eye for detail—he is the reason I can unconsciously calculate the statistical probability of a ragweed root's survival during any particular day in the New England growing season.

My mother: the artist, the teacher, the woman with the patience of a geological formation—she is the reason I can daydream away twelve hours, back bent, brown skin exposed to an August sun's ultraviolet assault. Did they know what they were doing? The facts of the case indicate premeditation. One does not marry one's polar opposite, buy a farm in rural Maine, till twenty acres of land, plant dry beans year after year, and then accidentally produce children with a natural talent for removing unwanted milkweed stalks.

There is no finer accomplishment than a clean row of soil, dark and rock-less, between two clumps of irrelevant verdure—soil a rake can comb with ease, unhindered by the sub-surface fingers of a blackberry root, or a mint shoot. Soil the color of molasses, weaving between kale stalks and tomato cages, announcing the way to move through a maze of greenery.

I have taken steps to hide this irksome disorder from friends and family. I have allowed the flowers greater and greater liberty within the confines of my plot, taken a zealously protective stance regarding volunteers of all inedible species. Small rings of colored rocks dot my giant plot, announcing the location of violets, daisies, and bachelor's buttons. To say "colored rocks" is perhaps misleading. These rings of soldier stones are not merely greys and whites, earth colored conglomerates one might come across on a nature walk. These rocks have been spray-painted vibrant reds, blues, purples, and yellows because such colors help accentuate their backdrop of deep brown soil.

I have spent a lifetime of summers bent in the task of clearing land. When not working on my parents' farm, I labored as a farm hand for our neighbors. I have weeded an onion patch for nine hours straight. Yes, there were water breaks and a brief hiatus for lunch, but the clock stopped for such dalliances. Nine hours was the time I wrote on my timecard. Nine hours kneeling in damp soil.

Strange things happen to skin when it knows soil so intimately. First, there is a caking. The dirt turns smooth, like an extra epidermal layer, an outer crust. Then, maybe four or six hours later, there is a fusion. The skin does not know where it begins or ends. The soil does not know either. When bent knees finally straighten, a cracking occurs, but nothing really moves. The body has joined the soil and even when washed, the skin stays dark. Brown flesh becomes dry when the air is dry and damp when the humidity rises. The body loses control over the soilskin, which is now an organism surviving without the oils and hydration of the rest of the body.

In my teenage years, I earned extra cash as a lowly employee of a non-competing local farm. It was there that I learned the futility of weeding in the rain. Pulling six-foot pigweed in a downpour is simply impossible. Dirt cannot be shaken free of roots when they are fat with moisture. Dirt clods in the rain. It clumps and balls and wads.

I could go on explaining the endless conditions in which I have weeded, or the many epiphanies I have experienced while hunched in a bean field, a carrot patch, or a cucumber grove. There is probably no such thing as a cucumber grove. I admit to taking liberties with agricultural lingo, this habit a product, no doubt, of my overdeveloped farm-ego. I could go on, but I find myself drifting, which is exactly what one must do when weeding. To weed is to slowly let go of the body. To weed is to let the body weed while the mind does something else entirely.

• • •

The rows of beans on the Freedom Farm were a quarter mile long, if I had to guess. Not much more than a two-foot space between them, and they covered acres and acres, varieties separated sometimes by a windrow of wheat or a sliver of bare soil. I walked back and forth hundreds of times, maybe thousands, while I lived under my parents' roof. We all did. Weeding was one of our mandatory contributions. It was paid work, a living wage (i.e., you live in this house and therefore you'll accept this wage), but I probably would have done it for free.

While my body weeded, I went traveling, and no matter where my imagination went, I was a more beautiful, talented, and desirable version of myself. I daydreamed with relentless verve and treasured the silence and space to be more than myself.

To weed is also to remember. Although it is true that most of my time was spent looking forward, there were hours spent going back—I had the time to work my memories down, to fine-tune and fiddle with their landscapes. While weeding, I could take it slow. I could recall over and over again until my memory's physical character mirrored its emotional content. It's too late now to worry, to regret what this process may have done to the authenticity of my recollections. I accept that I am predisposed to this kind of cultivation, pulling what is unnecessary so the rest can be seen. I accept that this is a too-tidy explanation for my version of the truth, but it is all I have.

For as long as I can remember, I have confidently explained the lifecycle of a weed to anyone who would listen. I have assured dozens and dozens of people that weed-seeds can remain dormant for seven years in the soil. But, if the land is weeded meticulously for seven years straight, the only weeds that will grow are those whose seeds blew in on a breeze, or were dropped by a passing bird. Seven years I've always said, and yet, I have no idea where I came up with this number. I have no reasonable guess as to how this arbitrary and very unlikely explanation of the weed-seed lifecycle latched on to my subconscious.

Is it wrong that I don't find this non-fact troubling in the least? I will continue repeating the seven-year weed cycle story because I find it oddly compelling. It strikes a chord with me—Mother Nature recognizing and rewarding persistence, granting order from chaos.

I recently took a personality test to determine what kind of worker I am. There were four different categories, and while I can't recite the specific implications of each, I do remember my classification: Banker/Lover. I am branded by the corporate world as a peacemaker who values order, and I am surprisingly onboard with this assessment. Even though I would not have named order as one of my values, the truth of it is undeniable. Order lends legitimacy to all of my values. Example: I value honesty. If I probe the surface of this value, if I investigate the reason for placing a premium on honesty, I discover that it serves to preserve order, it staves the entropic decay of relationships, communities, and cultures. The irony of valuing honesty while simultaneously propagating agricultural taradiddles is not lost on me.

No one is perfect.

There was milkweed, ragweed, chickweed, dandelion, pigweed, lambsquarter, white clover, hawkweed, and prostrate knotweed. There was the occasional vine bean needing to be pulled. Other farmers couldn't keep up. The weeds would get a couple weeks head start and there was nothing to be done. Entire crops of beans lost to the weed, but not on our farm. We had innate abilities, programmed success, undeniable advantage.

I was a cocky weeder. I'd say things like, "It's pretty simple. You just have to put in the time." And while this was true, it didn't quite add up. While I lived on our farm, I operated under this umbrella of superiority. I saw black and white because, in principle, that's how things are. There is right and there is wrong. There are weeds that need to be pulled. But what about farmers who didn't have four children well-versed in the rigors of manual labor? What about farmers who didn't have time, couldn't afford to pay someone else to do it, and couldn't do it themselves?

Weeders don't like to ask these questions. Weeders keep their heads down and work. We hope we never have to think about how complicated life is, how gray things get when "in principle" just doesn't apply. Weeders aren't really prepared for the world when they finally strike out on their own. It takes us some time to gain the perspective and humility required to wield our genetic predispositions responsibly.

Jenny at the end of a well-weeded row of beans.

Jenny learning to weed in her mother's garden.

The Night I Traveled
Through Time

The night I traveled through time was much like every other night. The Boys played their respective big brother roles with the same disdain and condescension as usual, Matthew was off on his own, probably building weapons, and our parents were going about their nightly routines.

If I'd known that I would be going to the future, I might have tried to enjoy the experience, but as is often the case with scientific discoveries, I was unaware at the time that anything out of the ordinary was happening.

I was a seventh grade scholar, intent on uncovering the relationship between sleep and our collective connection to the fabric of time. I'd been primed by years of PBS specials about black holes, wormholes, aliens, alternate realities and the space-time continuum. It didn't hurt that my father, a credible mathematician, had taken me into his confidence to discuss his nightly routine of sending out telepathic pleas for extraterrestrials to use him for medical experiments. My mother, who believed (a bit more sincerely) in the possibility of abduction, discouraged me from offering my own flesh in the name of science. If my father wanted to offer himself, that was one thing, but for him to deprive her of her children was quite another. It surprises me now to realize how long I held out hope, for my father's sake, that his pleas would be answered.

My three brothers and I lived with our parents in an old farmhouse on eighty acres of a hardscrabble farm. We were a curious clan, the kind that built things and broke things, lit fires to clear land, knocked bees' nests from tree limbs, and experimented with explosives. We were often willing to look into unconventional ideas for the sake of our own entertainment.

And despite their disagreement about whether I should allow my own abduction, both of my parents believed that encouraging unconventional thinking was an excellent method for producing well-rounded, freethinking children.

I was certainly a freethinker. Not in the sense that freethinkers make decisions and form opinions based on reason and fact, but in the way that my thoughts and ideas were generally free from the constraints of reality.

It was not unusual for me to fixate on scientific problems well beyond my comprehension. I suffered from the completely unfounded belief that I was capable of solving incredibly complex problems with little actual knowledge. I remember clearly the earliest of my projects, which was very well-received by a childhood friend, and so became a collaborative effort. Laura and I used some of her father's finest sheets of plywood to begin construction of a spaceship. We chose a private location to work, something out of the way, but also practical. A tree. We figured that if the spaceship never took its maiden voyage we would at least gain a tree house in the ordeal. The blueprints were extensive, as we were well aware that the planning phase was as important as the construction phase. I don't recall either of us being capable of using a saw, but I do remember spending a great deal of time painting a giant sheet of plywood wedged between two branches about ten feet above the ground. Laura's father wasn't pleased we'd taken liberties with his tools and materials, and the backlash led me to re-evaluate the prudence of scientific partnerships.

Then there was the four-month period spent pondering how one might include sun block in the production of common soap. This idea wasn't bad, but no matter how many times I drew a bar of soap and a tube of sunblock next to one another, I couldn't come up with the formula to make this invention possible.

There were self-cooking muffins, flying bikes, tree tents, refrigerators with invisible doors, and genetic manipulations of many sorts. The most amazing thing about my creative drive was my sincere belief that I could do the things I set out to do. I was genuinely surprised we didn't make it to space. I worried for years that someone else would invent sun block soap before I finished my calculations. My confidence was inspiring. But, I've digressed. Back to the night I traveled through time.

Having experienced waking moments similar, if not identical, to dreamed experiences, there was little doubt that my own subconscious was capable of interacting with time and space outside of the four accepted dimensions. Middle school science could not explain the need for sleep or the significance of dreams with any specificity, and so it became my mission to uncover the hidden secrets of time travel and the role of dreaming in its execution.

Several days prior to the night in question, I'd decided on a rudimentary, yet ambitious plan. In order to elucidate the connection between sleep and time, I would disrupt the former in the hope that something interesting would happen with the latter. I made no attempt to hide this plan from my brothers, but asked them as casually as possible to refrain from discussing my work in front of other, more conservative family members. Such an experiment would likely interfere with my health, or worse, my grades for a short time—a side effect I suspected my parents would not appreciate.

I will be the first to admit that my under-standing of the scientific method—in particular, the existence of controlled variables and hypotheses—was limited, but what I lacked in knowledge I made up in sheer enthusiasm.

My brother Jason was incredulous at my curiosity. Of all the laws to question, I'm sure he found it ludicrous that I chose scientific principles above cultural and political norms. Luis, too, was disapproving. When he caught wind of my intention to investigate covertly he was confounded that the one time I chose to sneak around, I sought no tangible reward for my efforts.

As a teenager, Luis's world was small; it began in his eyes and ended about four feet from his body in every direction, sometimes slightly farther, depending on the location of the nearest girl. Jason, on the other hand, insisted that his perception of the world was irrelevant because life had no intrinsic value or meaning. While Luis rarely interfered with my daily activities, Jason took personal responsibility for crushing my optimism, which according to him was a maladjusted behavior for an adolescent to exhibit.

Thankfully, I have always been able to overcome great quantities of negativity. My desire to understand the link between dreams and time travel could not be squelched. I was raised to pursue curiosities with relentless vigor and intended to have answers of one kind or another.

The experiment began on a school night,

a choice for which I cannot fully recollect the reasoning. I do, however, recall the thrill of beginning such an undertaking with an unapproved, underage human test subject (me). The risks of interfering with my connection to the fabric of time were incalculable, but for the betterment of mankind and following in the footsteps of countless brave medical researchers before me, I donated myself to the cause.

Somewhere in the middle of the first night, Jason pushed the bedroom door open and peeked his head in. Undoubtedly, the expression on my pale face, lit by the glowing yellow light of my bedside lamp, said "guilty." I am not now, nor have I ever been, blessed with the ability to fain casual indifference in the face of anything at all. What was I guilty of? With older siblings, there does not need to be a clearly defined crime to elicit a feeling of guilt. Siblings make guesses about unusual behavior and often report these guesses as fact to parents, hoping for a good fight. I was guilty of doing something my older brother did not understand.

Jason fancied himself a philosopher and I was convinced this made it impossible for us to agree on matters of hard science. There didn't seem much point in discussing my activities, so I dismissed his sneer with a wave of my hand.

It should be noted that due to the nature of the experiment, my recollections of conversations occurring during that time are mediocre at best. If Jason spoke to me that night, I'm sure he used discouraging words like "idiotic," "aneurism," "psychosis," and "permanent." He was prone to hyperbole.

Aside from Jason's brief castigation, the first night passed without incident. Adrenaline fueled my quiet steps back and forth across the worn floorboards and despite feeling a little sick to my stomach I was ready for the day.

While at school I suffered minor discomfort, but managed to maintain my composure. I pretended to take notes in class and kept under the radar at lunch, nodding amiably as friends chatted to either side of me. I went about my afternoon routine as usual, consuming an appalling quantity of Oreo cookies while watching reruns of *Star Trek*. I did my homework before dinner and then whatever chore I had been assigned. Without being too obvious, I took special precautions to avoid excessive contact with my mother, an incredibly vigilant woman. I would have much preferred an inquisitive mother, one who asked a lot of questions but lacked intuition. My mother, however, knew the futility of questioning a pre-teen. She had been primed by The Boys, and was now eerily evolved, capable of detecting slight disturbances in her children's behavior.

In truth, I don't remember much about my second night of sleeplessness. I probably watched a lot of TV. Maybe I re-evaluated my reasons for undertaking the experiment, or outlined a series of target experiences, but probably not. I'd like to report that I had specific questions in need of answers, or theories in need of proofs, but most likely, I just wanted something unexpected to happen. Something exciting.

The Boys each checked in on me before going off to bed and though neither said as much, they were both clearly unimpressed with my withering faculties. It didn't surprise me that they had joined forces. Regularly at odds with one another, they managed to function remarkably well when unified against a common threat. More often than not, I was that threat.

Trying to function when your body has missed *two* entire nights of sleep is madness. During the second day of wakefulness, my teachers became visibly concerned, prolonged eye contact, probing questions, and sympathetic lip puckers followed me through the halls. Even Mrs. Hubbard, who was no stranger to my scientific ambitions, having had to request on several occasions that I refrain from holding my breath during her lectures (to test and improve lung capacity), was alarmed at my inability to participate in class.

It was all I could do to climb the steps of Mrs. Woodberry's bus for the ride home. My legs felt leaden, my eyelids burned, and it felt as though my stomach had relocated to somewhere much lower and less comfortable within my abdomen. By the time the bus dropped me off at home, I was too tired to remember why I had chosen to stay awake in the first place. I didn't care if time existed, let alone time travel.

I was the first one home that afternoon; the boys played sports and my mother and father didn't finish work for several hours. Somehow as my fifty-eight hours of wakefulness came to a close, I managed to find my bed.

When I awoke, my arms and legs were heavy with exhaustion, and my spirit slightly bruised at the lack of scientific advancement despite my effort. I had no recollection of dreams, nor had I experienced any disruption in linear time.

I exited my bedroom at the top of the stairs just as Jason reached the landing. Feeling somewhat defeated and defensive of my choice to undergo what had amounted to little more than torture, I lashed out when I saw his smug face and irksome irreverence for the scientific method.

I have never asked Jason, but have always suspected that he knew from the moment our eyes met in the stairwell of my imminent jump through the space-time continuum. "You look like hell," he offered, "and Mum is doing the dishes because you went to bed without doing your chores. Real nice."

As I'm sure Jason was aware, neglecting chores was cause for great guilt, and so, despite near crippling exhaustion, I rushed downstairs and inserted myself beside my mother at the sink. "I've got these, Mum. Sorry I didn't do them last night."

Instead of being grateful, as I expected, her shoulders lifted and tightened as her head dropped ever so slightly, a decidedly feline posture I'd come to recognize and fear. She was on the hunt. For what, I didn't know. Her movements became painfully slow as she dried her hands and stepped away from the sink, "Okaay," the word stretched from her lips and hung between us. I turned away from her but could feel her eyes narrowing, the uncomfortable tingle of parental scrutiny on my back. The window above the sink, still dark so early in the morning, held her reflection, unduly cautious.

I knew better than to run, hide, or acknowledge her heightened awareness, so I went back to rinsing soapy mugs and plates while my mother lowered herself to a stool at the counter and opened a book. When I finished, I left my mother in the kitchen and went to brush my teeth, change clothes, and wet my hair so that I could braid it for school.

Five minutes later, as I emerged from the bathroom, Jason walked past, into the kitchen. Mum was still sitting at the counter, reading her latest crime thriller like it was the most natural thing in the world to be pleasure reading at five thirty in the morning. When she saw me, she looked at Jason, then back to me and asked, "Where do you think you're going?"

"What?"

"Where are you going?" she asked again, her suspicion deepening. I had no idea what was happening, so I eyed *her* with even greater suspicion, a defense tactic I'd picked up from watching Jason. Neither of us spoke for a long time, each of us trying to identify why exactly the situation so confused the other. I walked over to her and felt her forehead. "Mum, are you feeling alright?"

Jason walked up next to me and felt her forehead too, an uncharacteristically kind gesture for him. At this, my mother slammed her book on the counter and left the room, muttering under her breath that the two of us were up to something.

It was nearing six, and I hadn't started packing my bag, so instead of engaging Jason, who was staring with unsettling satisfaction, I made my lunch, ate a bowl of cereal, and collected my books.

Luis walked into the kitchen, raised an eyebrow in my direction, then grabbed a cookie from the jar and walked back to the living room.

Jason sat quietly at the counter, observing me with what was beginning to look like mirth. "What the heck is going on?" I growled. His shoulders shrugged noncommittally.

I stormed past him, into the living room where my mother and Luis sat on the couch watching the news. Jason stood quickly and followed close behind, appearing both interested and detached.

Inserting myself between the television and the couch, hands on hips, I began the interrogation. I wanted to know why I was the only one getting ready, why my mother was acting so strange, why Jason was watching me, and why Luis was eating cookies for breakfast.

Before anyone could answer, my father stepped from his office wearing sweat pants and a T-shirt, a carved walnut pipe tucked at the corner of his mouth. My father was an unconventional man, but smoking a pipe at six in the morning was beyond comprehension. He asked, "What's the commotion?"

I stood frozen in place, eyes darting from one face to another. They all stared back.

The wooden clock shaped like the state of Maine that hung above our couch grew louder in the silence. Each step of the second hand marched more deliberately, the ratcheting gears slowing to a hypnotizing crawl.

I turned to face my father.

"What time is it?"

He was the only one I trusted in practical matters, the only one too busy to bother with tricks and deception.

He looked up at the state of Maine and then to

me. "It's . . ." and as he began to say the words, I understood, ". . . sixteen past six."

"Oh," I said, my face flushing, "I'm going to bed early tonight. I'm exhausted."

My mother looked relieved, Luis looked at the TV, and my father went back to smoking his pipe. Jason, who had known all along that I had crawled from bed at five thirty in the evening thinking it was the next morning, stepped up beside me and said, "Goodnight."

As I made my way up the stairs, I heard Jason explaining to my mother what had happened. He laughed harder than he'd ever laughed before, and maybe since. My mother laughed too. Just as I reached the top step, I heard my father cut in, "It sounds to me like she did exactly what she aimed to do."

I was too embarrassed and exhausted at the time to appreciate it, but my father was right. For just over forty minutes, I'd been living in the future.

The Snare Years

Imagine using a spoon to fling food across the room—the food sits in the dip of the cupped end and a finger pulls it back while the other hand grips the handle and puts tension on the length of the spoon. When the cupped end is released, the food is flung into the air. Now imagine a wooden spoon four inches in diameter and forty feet long. Instead of food, imagine the cup end as a loop of twine meant to snag a perpetrator's ankle. This was my younger brother's final snare, the culmination of three years of experimentation and diligent study.

This trap was an attempt to deter me from a fortress, or rather, the tangled branches and brambles of our family's overgrown cemetery. The four-inch-thick spoon was, in reality, the trunk of a birch tree. I can only speculate at the details of the snare's construction, but it probably took hours to bend the tip of that young birch from sky to ground. My brother Matthew must have borrowed a pulley from our father's boat rigging supplies because the force required to tame the birch was far greater than such a small boy could have mustered on his own. The trunk was no less than four inches at the base and tapered to a diameter similar to that of my adolescent wrists. Matthew had notched a wedge in a stump just beneath the top of the bent birch. He made a loop in one end of a thick rope and tied the other around the tip of the prostrate tree. Once secure, he hooked the looped end into the stump's wedge to lock it in place. The tension kept the rope taught and the birch tree ready to explode upward upon release.

Perhaps some background is required: Because he was a lover of all weapons, the deadlier the better, Matthew's youth was marked by the continuous and oft alarming advancements in his craftsmanship. It makes sense to me now, his fascination with self-defense. It was an arms race. As my older brothers and I grew bigger and stronger, Matthew developed progressively sophisticated methods of promoting his own well-being.

It started with cast-plaster, the malleable white material used in constructing splints and casts. Matthew's source was a local nurse, the mother of one of his friends, who found his interest in crafting reproductions of ancient weaponry charming. If she suspected his implements would be used in real-life confrontations, she never let on. She gave him unrestricted access to the material, and was a little too liberal with her suggestions for improvement, if you ask me.

When he got tired of the jagged edge of a sword or scythe, Matthew would heat the material in boiling water and shape it into a throwing star, mace, or whatever weapon had piqued his interest that week. Often ideas came from the hardcover picture book of medieval weapons that our mother, for reasons beyond comprehension, had provided him.

It didn't take long for Matthew to realize the limited capabilities of his plaster morning star clubs, falchions, and war hammers. He'd grown old enough to use a whittling knife and so began manufacturing spears and arrows, collecting triangular rocks from the bean fields and using other stones to chip and sharpen them into arrowheads and spear tips.

I wonder now whether Matthew's obvious upper hand when it came to causing bodily harm is what provoked The Boys and I to find unique methods of wreaking havoc on his developing mind. Older siblings tend to think it their duty to "teach lessons," and when these lessons cannot be taught with the aid of physical threat, there is an inevitable shift to more psychologically subtle tactics.

I hesitate to provide an example.

Matthew was a trusting boy. He took the word of our parents as undeniable fact. This may not seem like a negative trait, but in our house, thinking for oneself was of paramount importance. Discovering and standing for truth came above familial ties, and it was expected that we each use our own deductive reasoning to uncover the nature of things, regardless of what we were told. At least, this is the lesson I identify post-factum in the story I am about to recount.

When Matthew was four or five years old, like many children of that age, he inquired about the day he was born. Unfortunately for him, he chose to lodge his inquiry with the wrong department. My father, generally pleased with Matthew's level of curiosity and ingenuity, decided to go along with, instead of discredit, a wildly inaccurate tale, whose origin I will not mention.

Matthew was regaled with a fantastic and horrifically offensive birth story. Our father may not have conceived the tale, but he did much to strengthen its integrity. As I recall, it began with a dark and stormy night in February of 1983. Winters in Maine can be difficult for transients, and Matthew's mother was just such an individual. I use the word "individual" deliberately, as the word "person" would not be accurate. You see, Matthew's biological mother was an extraterrestrial. More specifically, she was a Klingon. For those not versed in *Star Trek* speciation, a Klingon is marked by a set of homely forehead ridges. This fact may have detracted from the believability of the story had our father not insisted that Matthew's father was human, and the ridges were passed down only from the paternal Klingon line.

The Klingon woman knocked at our door late in the evening, asking for a place to sleep. My parents were uncomfortable allowing a foreigner to stay in the house, so offered her the loft in our barn. At this point, when Matthew might have begun to correlate his own birth with something more divine, the story took a turn for the ugly. The woman gave birth, unbeknownst to us—and prior to sneaking off into the night, placed her half-human babe into a freshly formed pile of dung, to keep him warm until morning.

This is how my parents found him, snuggled comfortably in the sticky excrement of our dairy cows. They took him in, and the rest was history.

In a surprising twist, Matthew was delighted by his half-human status. He had a particular fondness for Klingons and was grateful that his "real" mother had loved him enough to leave him with a relatively good family. There is no doubt in my mind that as soon as our mother discovered that Matthew had been misled, she attempted to correct the situation. It was too late. Despite knowing, on some level, that he was not the half-breed bastard son of a homeless Klingon, Matthew chose to continue believing. In hindsight, the pleasure he derived from this farcical birth story is a little disheartening. Did he feel so much an outsider that the story validated his suspicion of otherness?

This was the way with Matthew. We would

attempt a con, hoping to prove his gullibility, naiveté, or ignorance, and he would somehow turn the tables—not with anger or sadness, but with sincerity. I picked on Matthew for years, and don't remember ever feeling satisfaction at the task. I dropped fake spiders on his body (to help him overcome his irrational arachnophobia), hid his favorite weapons, and relentlessly teased him. He was an impossible mark—above it in a way that I still don't understand.

In fact, I wonder what I might have done in the days or even weeks leading up to the final snare to provoke Matthew. This detail is oddly absent from my memory, but I would not be surprised to learn that I deserved some form of payback.

Even so, I am thankful that the final snare came to my attention prior to its first deployment. I don't recall what alerted me to the danger, but I would guess the bent birch's uncomfortable creaking may have tipped me off. Matthew lay in wait, crouched behind a nearby tree or perhaps draped in its branches. I called to him to reveal himself, admitting, though I found his intentions deplorable, that I respected the artistry of his invention. We spent several minutes admiring his handiwork together. This admiration served two purposes. First, I learned how best to identify similar traps in the future by examining the materials and their placement. Second, I was able to use flattery to divert my brother's aggression and convince him of the need to perform an inanimate object test-run prior to human trials.

There had been a lot of scary steps between Matthew's cast plaster days and that day in the cemetery, namely, those occurring within the three-year period between Matthew's ninth and twelfth birthdays. I call these the Snare Years. It was a dangerous time around the farm for people and animals alike.

Many of Matthew's snares had been tested with household objects, but unfortunately, some had been deployed in unanticipated circumstances.

The Snare Years started innocently enough. Our father began insisting that the only way to catch a skunk was with a live trap. Until one's house, pet, or car has been sprayed, it is impossible to fully comprehend how ludicrous this tactic is, but with a little imagination, most people come close. It might have been irritating, my father's constant need to prove some kind of dominance over, or maybe it was kinship with the animal kingdom, had he not, time and time again, been correct in his assertion that the animal in question would not harm him or his property. He assured the family that if treated properly, with respect, the skunks would not spray when caught.

Matthew was immediately on board with the concept of live-trapping, and took the work seriously. He and my father began experimenting with different kinds of bait: peanut butter, granola bars, slabs of meat, scrambled egg, who knows what they slid into that live trap. The problem was that nothing was working. During this same period, Matthew began focusing his energy on learning the art of the leg snare, the most cinematically pleasing of live-trapping techniques.

In hindsight, someone should have realized that Matthew's obsession with leg snares and his tireless pursuit of the ideal skunk-bait would intersect. A leg snare is not the ideal way to detain a creature with pheromone ejection capabilities, but the prospect of getting a good look at one of these illusive creatures likely overpowered my younger brother's underdeveloped common sense.

For weeks my father had been trying to convince me that feeding my Maine Coon cat, Precious, outside of the garage would alleviate our late-night skunk problem. One skunk in particular had taken a liking to the cat food, and for several nights in a row had been surprised by one of us on our way to the woodpile after dark. Luckily, no one had been sprayed, but we were playing a dangerous game. Upon hearing that skunks enjoyed Purina brand cat food, Matthew began hatching a plan that did not take into consideration the implications of using cat food as skunk bait.

I was not present when Precious was

discovered. No one but Matthew knew where the snare was set, but when he found my poor feline dangling by a front paw, he ran straight to our father. For good reason, he was horrified that his attempt to catch a skunk had resulted in tragedy—one that would put him at great risk of sibling retaliation. Our father wasn't particularly distraught as he cut the cat from her binding. He must have surmised that the damage was not fatal because his reaction was one of amusement and not condemnation.

I was informed of the incident rather insensitively. As I passed the scene of the crime, our father waved me over to share his deconstruction of Matthew's leg-hold snare design with what sounded like pride. Instead of reprimanding my brother for injuring a family pet, he was complimenting his son for his initiative and unique style. Matthew had unintentionally solved our skunk problem. With the cat now terrified of cat food, it was no longer necessary to leave dishes of Purina in the garage.

By the age of twelve, Matthew had learned a few tricks. He'd had some experience with pulleys, understood the concept of leverage, and had learned his way around our father's workshop, which contained every tool a boy could dream of.

Like many of my memories, the day of the last snare is fuzzy. I view my recounting as more of a representation, a palimpsest of nostalgia, than a factual regurgitation. For me, memories are like this—aggregates of emotional impressions, facts, and imagination, but this makes them no less real. They are, in many ways, more truthful than the events themselves.

Matthew's last snare was a tribute to the form, and in all honesty, rather spectacular. He agreed to throw a log into the loop of rope, which was covered hastily by leaves and small sticks.

To say we were surprised by the speed of the log's ascent would be an understatement. I have no idea how much our test log weighed, but at the time, I was convinced that my own weight couldn't have been more than twice that of our inanimate victim's. Before either of us could scream our shock, the log was gone. It should be noted that the original intent of the snare was not to release its prey. Matthew had imagined my limp but unharmed body hanging by an ankle from the top of the tree, however the fraying twine he'd used had been incapable of tolerating the forces involved. At the very moment the twine was needed most, as the log reached the outer limits of its trajectory, it snapped. The log became airborne, flying well over the tops of nearby trees and making its way over the rock wall.

I've never attempted to pinpoint the moment that Matthew shifted from an aggressor to a protector, but it may have been that day in the cemetery. I have a feeling that it was his first glimpse of my mortality, of his ability to drastically alter the course of our family's story. At first the change was almost imperceptible, small kindnesses extended in my direction, confessions of past digressions and apologies for cold-hearted deeds I'd never even been aware of. But before long, Matthew and I were soldiers fighting together, facing our adolescence with pluck and kinship.

To this day, there is no doubt in my mind that Matthew's final snare would have flung me to my death.

He was really quite talented.

The Memory Box

The lulling growl of my first car's German engine kept me company through the August night. It was a short drive from the new house to the Freedom Farm. When I pulled into the driveway, I turned the headlights off and let the car roll to a stop. Starlight seen through several cracks in the cloud cover, cast a splotchy glow on the splintered white of ancient shingles.

The air was still except for the occasional chirp of a wind chime my mother had forgotten in the bobbing branch of a lilac bush, its metal fingers the dangling tines of an abandoned tuning fork. The house was silent, waiting without protest for its new family, the one that would arrive in a few short hours, to claim it.

Stepping from the car I made my way to the garage's carport door. Its brown slats pulled tight to the pavement were, for the first time, an uninviting sight. The familiar musk of damp cement and maple bark at the back of my throat, I worked my way through a landscape of cardboard boxes, garbage bags, and children's toys. The new owners had started filling the garage with their things, too excited to wait until we were completely gone. The cool metal knob of the hallway door rattled gently—a hushed sound, like a paper bag being tossed by the wind—as it met my fingers in the dark. How many times had I reached for it, eyes open wide, yet seeing nothing? How often in the years we'd lived here had I tiptoed past the bicycles, kindling piles, and cat food bowls, to stealthily make my way to the bedroom at the top of the stairs? I no longer needed the dim glow of a flickering bulb to light the way. Navigating this house, its doors with too-tight springs, creaking floorboards, and awkward angles, was muscle memory.

When I was born, my mother bought a pink, cardboard filing box; delicate flowers were printed along the length of its collapsible sides. In it she placed the fine curls from my first haircut and the lacey white baptismal gown I wore in St. Augustine's church when I was a few months old. There were pictures, newspaper clippings, and samples of my work from each grade in elementary school. She called it my memory box. I used to peruse its contents from time to time, admiring the objects within. These things had touched me in some way, held meaning.

At first only my mother chose items worth saving, but eventually I was trusted with adding to the box as I saw fit. Favorite swaths of cloth cut from well-worn shirts and dresses, stuffed animals, love letters, journals, and beloved pieces of jewelry filled the box to its brim.

Walking through the hallway door of my childhood home, I felt unwelcomed. The home I had always known no longer existed. The hall door swung inward, its brown paint worn through to white where our hands had propped it open. My brothers and I had taken turns, one holding the door while the other carried teetering piles of wood to fill the box. Five armfuls for The Boys would last us one New England night, but for me it had always taken seven. This hallway was the place we stood tall each September, waiting for Mum to mark our height with a pencil in the molding.

I expected to catch the familiar scent of chainsaw grease, salty work clothes, or a hint of sweetness from pears ripening on the sill, but instead, the clinical sting of bleach burned my nostrils. The air felt thin as I stepped through it, lonely like hospitals and waiting rooms. Beyond this passageway lay the kitchen, its door freshly painted white to match the smooth ceramic handle. This was the handle that Pa had threatened to tie my front teeth to, threatened to tie all of our teeth to, at one time or another.

I lifted each foot in an exaggerated motion over the doorjamb, also freshly painted. The kitchen was hollow, a seashell without an echo. No stools propped beneath the island counter, no dining table, or rocking chair with woven rug beneath

103

its runners. My mother had rocked back and forth in that chair with each of us, whispering in our ears, "Ahh ah ah ah," her voice rising slightly every fourth breath. The photo collage of 1996, the last year we were all together, no longer hung on the far wall. There were no pots and pans, no teakettle, and no collection of my father's pipes on the old hutch. We had stripped the house bare, taken ourselves out for good.

I have a friend whose home was destroyed by fire. She lost everything. I didn't have the heart to ask whether she'd had a memory box like mine, but I thought about it for weeks after learning of her loss. I was devastated for her, but also, I couldn't let go of the fear, a lingering panic at my own vulnerability. Not a physical vulnerability or concern for my health or wellbeing, but a crisis of sentimentality. So many of my memories are linked to objects, to items for which I have no particular fondness, but am incapable of discarding.

And what is the difference—because I know there is one—between a house burned down and a house abandoned? Is a leaving behind somehow less permanent than a taking away? It's true that I can always go back. I can walk Greeley Road and stare at the old property, wondering what the insides of our farmhouse might look like now. I could even knock on their door, if I really wanted to, and ask for a tour. But I won't.

I stood, back to the kitchen door, hands still clasping the handle behind me, stuck. It felt like an open casket funeral, a look into the grey skin of a dead friend. I couldn't bring myself to walk the empty rooms, or to climb the old staircase. I couldn't bring myself to touch the pink rose wallpaper of my parents' bedroom, or open my father's suit and tie closet one last time. I didn't turn on the lights or flush the toilets; I didn't taste the well water or open the fridge.

I slid, body pressed to the wall, to the office door tucked just to the right of the woodstove. Still facing the bare kitchen, I opened the door and side-stepped into the cool darkness of my father's office. This was the reason I had come.

Hundreds of vaguely sour-smelling books, their jaundiced paper having started to turn, stood back to back, abandoned. Philosophy, theology, physics, classic literature, poetry, calculus, all left behind.

My father, had he known what I intended, would have called me foolish, needlessly nostalgic. He would have argued that the books had no value beyond the information contained within them. He would've said, "If you don't read them, they're worthless."

I knew I would never read them. I hadn't come to rescue knowledge. Most of the physics books were outdated; the theology and poetry books were of no particular interest to me, and the calculus was above my understanding.

That these things were books mattered little. It could have been maps, tools, or a piece of furniture. It was that they belonged to this place, my father's office. They were the physical manifestation of every story that ever began or ended in that office. The books reminded me of the rust-orange carpet beneath my feet. A carpet I spent hours kneeling on, searching for BBs and extracting them between forefinger and thumb from thick shag. It never struck me as odd, that there were so many, always more and more and more. But now I wonder if my father dropped them on purpose, a clever tactic to entertain a chronically busy child.

The rug reminded me of the painting that sat on an easel in the corner, a portrait of a white-bearded man, a familiar stranger. My father painted him and left him to rest for over a decade on the easel, overlooking his desk. The desk reminded me of the open closet, full of my mother's largest pots and pans, picnic baskets, and other too-large kitchen implements.

The closet reminded me of the small metal door beside my father's desk attached to the backside of the chimney. My father opened it to slide a tilted mirror into the brick column to inspect for creosote. The books are a reminder of a thousand other reminders, a small block in the foundation of memory.

I am afraid of forgetting. No, that's not quite right. I'm afraid of losing those things that help me remember. My father's books, that office, the potbelly woodstove, the kitchen sink with pipes that froze, the upstairs closets with bins of winter clothes, the wooden floorboards of my childhood room, the living room rug, the giant jar of coins at the base of the stairs—to me, these things are sacred. And even though I have lost their box, here they are in words. Words are the only ever-lasting container. Ever—a strange word in itself—conveying timelessness, as in, at all times, always. Or in the way that ever doesn't matter after we are gone.

Someday I may lose my father's books. I may lose my pink filing box and the stack of twenty journals I have piled on top of it. So I write. I write about the old house, the books, the shingles, the wallpaper, the floorboards, the rocking chair, and the stove. I write in the hope that words have more power than things, that they will last at least as long as I do.

I carried every book from that office to my car. I stacked them as high as they would go in the front and back seats, piled them neatly in the trunk, and wedged them between the windshield and the dash. When I was done, I stepped out of my shoes and tiptoed through the wet grass to collect my mother's wind chime from the thin branch of a lilac bush.

Drifting Without Beans

I grew up as a member of a secret society.

We were bean farmers.

I can identify the leaves of bean plants at sixty miles an hour from the back seat of a car. I recognize the smell of unripe pods as they stretch in the sun, a scent thick as paste at the back of your throat, rich and bitter like a blend of raw almond and fresh blades of grass. I've been buried up to the neck in beans. I've eaten cold bean salad, baked beans, bean burgers, refried beans, boiled beans, bean loaf, bean-paste cookies, and bean ice cream. I know over two-dozen dry bean varieties by sight. I can tell you that Marafax are some of the best for baking, and that Black Turtle, Calypso, and Jacob's Cattle are the most visually pleasing. Calypsos are a miniature hugging Yin and Yang, Jacob's Cattle are a white with reddish spots, and Black Turtle are sleek panthers that make their way into soup mixes all over New England. I'm not bragging—this is more of a confession. My whole life I have struggled to maintain and recall accurate, detailed memories of events and people. But for reasons I cannot explain, I have never forgotten a bean.

• • •

The New Year always began in spring. A battle with the earth itself, rocks pushed forth from the depths, an upward swelling of soil. We were dedicated soldiers in a never-ending battle. The rocks had to be removed if beans were to be planted. Six of us and the tractor made seven, going from acre to acre clearing the largest rocks with our bare hands; throwing them, if we could, into the tractor's bucket as it passed.

Once in a while our digging fingers couldn't pry a stone from its resting place. Pa would grab the crow bar and we'd gather, hoping this time it would be the big one. There was a special place for the big ones, a spot tucked just outside of view from the road. In the twenty years we picked rocks, only three made the cut. Stones larger than the tractor's back tires. Stones worked back and forth, pushed, pulled, wedged, rolled. Heavier than a car.

And when the Yellow Eye or Cranberry made their way to soil, I had no doubt they'd grow. If the dirt could push granite from the ledge below, how could it fail to support the weight of these tiny beans?

September saw beans dying on their stalks and this was what we wanted. Brown and brittle pods were easily shucked by a combine. But first, the plants had to be pulled from the earth. Six

The old Freedom barn.

rows into one, without losing their precious cargo. For this, we woke before the sun. The five of us rolled from our beds, wrapped our bodies in flannel and wool, slid our feet into boots and made our way to the machinery shed. Luis and I arrived first, grinning at the bite of autumn air in our throats, we've always been morning people. Jason and Matthew took longer to walk the two hundred feet from the garage door to the shed, dragging their feet, grimacing at the task ahead. There, leaning against the pine planks of the shed wall, our pitchforks waited, splintered handles damp with dew, rusted tines bent awkwardly with use. The tractor purred in the distance, our father atop it, glancing back every few feet to ensure the bean-puller blades were catching the roots just so.

The stalks too were covered with dew, and that is why we rose so early. Moisture softened the beans and their pods just enough to prevent cracks, just enough to keep our Yellow Eye and King's Early within their protective sheaths. We knew where to place our pitchforks, how to lift tangled heaps of Soldier and Cranberry from one place to another forming golden rows in the pre-dawn light. We did it every fall for as long as we could remember.

We worked until it was done. Our beans lay drying in the sun, waiting for the shimmying fingers of the combine to comb them up.

In winter our work was of a different kind. The bean room was a roughly finished rectangular space in our barn. As thick as the walls and made from the same raw plywood and insulating foam, when closed, the door was nearly invisible. If our secret society had a sacred place, this was it. We gathered here most nights, sometimes for as little as ten minutes and others for stretches as long as three hours. On the left side of the room, reaching almost to the ceiling was a large metal bean-filled bin. It was gravity fed through a metal tube from a 1000-pound capacity storage bin in the loft above. At the base of the lower bin was a long and narrow opening that clicked and tapped in rhythm with the slow churn of a black conveyor belt. The conveyor was almost six feet long and just over a foot wide, running through the center of the room. It was flanked on both sides by a wooden trough for tossing culls, rocks, bugs and any other detritus passing by. The bean machine sat six comfortably; three on each side, tasked with ensuring our beans were clean and ready for sale. As we sat, straight-backed on our wooden benches, the belt rolled by, littered with beans fresh from our fields. My parents, always at the end of the line, were the final inspectors before our product fell into the open mouth of a burlap sack.

I am part of another family now: my own. I have a husband, two sons, and a daughter and we are drifting without beans. I find myself, for the first time, nervous at the prospect of wandering so aimlessly into the future. Not for myself, but for my children. Without beans, how will they remember these years, the ones that are now passing too quickly?

Beans were the framework to which my memory fastened detail. Because of beans, I am able to recall with clarity the way that early morning fog clung in tiny droplets to the invisible hairs on my cheeks as I walked the rows with a pitchfork. Beans were my catalyst, the thing from which sensory memories grew.

As spring arrives, I find myself once again scouring checkout lines for seed packets with pictures of kale, spinach, and rainbow chard. I can see my garden taking shape even before the seeds have touched soil. The sunflowers line the fence like always, salad greens in diagonals, and there are beans in neatly spaced, ten-foot rows.

Maybe this year I'll plant Marafax beans, round and orange. Come fall, their pods, bleached by the sun and crisp from the heat, will pop. I can already see my children's little fingers, nails like black crescent moons, packed with soil, scraping beans from the brittle backbones of their sheaths.

PART TWO

PALERMO, MAINE
2015-2019

Our new old barn.

The Second Sort

One fall morning, I looked on Craigslist for goats. I'd been thinking about goats for two or three days, which had been sufficient time to convince myself that I would make a very fine goat farmer indeed. I pictured myself milking them and then making cheese with the milk. They would be gentle and playful and I would brush their fur when it became matted so that it might remain pristine for sheering once a year. I would be spinning by that time, well-practiced and efficient as I transformed our crop of wool into yarn.

My husband may have heard me musing about goats, but didn't take me seriously for any number of reasons. He wasn't much for idle chatter about animals we didn't own and work we didn't know how to do. He's very practical in that way. He went off to work that morning, waving goodbye, pecking my cheek, assuming that everything would be pretty much the same when he returned that evening.

As soon as he was gone, I hopped into the car with his younger brother Tyler, who I'd met only a few times before, and who was visiting for the week. Tyler seemed pleased to be on a covert mission, one that had the potential to disrupt his older brother's equilibrium. We drove for almost two hours, farther and farther into the Washington countryside. When we arrived at the muddy drive of a family desperately in need of fewer animals and more space, my hopes began to rise. A young girl, who may or may not have been licensed to drive, jumped into a pick-up and asked us to follow her to an off-site enclosure.

When we arrived, the pen was empty, a fact that might have discouraged the fainter of heart (and more sensible). For me, the distant ringing of alarm bells was an invitation to proceed. The goats, which were presented as an unverified pygmy breed, had escaped and run half a mile into the woods. The salesgirl, apparently unfazed, led us to the spot she thought they might be grazing. Sure enough, there they were. Five or six of these horrendously matted creatures, whose physiques, I would later learn, make them impossible to milk.

The young girl had a bizarre conviction that the only way her goats would be happy, the two she had for sale, was if they were sold together.

I chose not to inform her that, despite my sincere interest in these animals, I was neither equipped nor inclined to concern myself with a goat's emotional well-being. They were both female, a mother-daughter pair, and I was so intoxicated by the idea of cheese and wool and the genial relationship I imagined myself having with these animals, that I didn't balk. I offered to take both, as though it had always been my plan. I dislike admitting it, but it seems obvious now that the little sales shark was more talented than I gave her credit for. I can say with certainty that these goats were not happier together. She, on the other hand, was likely *much* happier having rid herself of not one, but two of the miserable creatures.

In my mind, there are two types of farmers. Those who spend countless hours obsessing over the imminent arrival of their domesticated charges and those in whom the reality of animal husbandry does not strike until the moment their newly acquired pygmies jump from the sullied trunk of a two-door Honda Civic. I am the second sort.

I often tell myself that this chronic lack of preparation is related to my sense of adventure— a joy-seeking impulse—but, upon putting it to paper, I feel pressed to admit a certain level of laziness. My father, a far shrewder farmer than I, used to tell me that necessity was the mother of invention, and though it was likely not his intent, the old proverb instilled in me a poor habit of waiting for necessity.

My father likes to tell an appalling story to illustrate the importance of diligence on the farm, one that vilifies those who make a habit of waiting for necessity. While I'm quite certain he told it as a cautionary tale, I never saw it that way.

Doug Hoult was a pig farmer and an acquaintance of my father's. His house smelled like pigs. His clothes smelled like pigs. His hair smelled like pigs. The entire plot he lived on, a substantial acreage, smelled like pigs. One might assume that any man willing to endure this odiferous profession would have to be an expert, a man making significant profits, a man well versed in the affairs of the hog. Not so. Doug Hoult, despite his experience, hadn't castrated two of his largest boars. Even I, a novice, can tell you that there is a very good reason for the early separation of a male pig with his parts—boar taint. This is a form of meat contamination caused by the deposit of testicular pheromones (among other things) in the animal's fat. Boar taint means foul tasting meat and poor cash return when the animal is brought to market. In fact, as my father remembers it, the year Hoult asked him to castrate the two 600-pound boars, barrow meat went for forty-nine cents a pound and boar went for twenty-three.

In the years after my parents moved to town, my father had cultivated his reputation as a bold, slightly unstable, and competent farmer. A man who, when necessity arose, always conquered with invention. My father is and was an honest man, and although it might appear he was willing to take part in a scam (the last-minute castration of hogs already quite contaminated with the taint), I think his willingness to be complicit in such an ordeal can be otherwise explained. Technically the meat would be barrow meat. Technically there were no rules being broken. If the individual who chose to pay barrow price did not first inspect the undercarriage of his or her hog, was it not their fault? Carelessness is a businessman's downfall. It was never discussed, but I suspect that part of my father's willingness to aid Hoult stemmed from a desire to help a struggling farmer. Hoult was going to attempt this nonsense whether my father was there or not. And if he hadn't been, Hoult might have been killed trying to raise a few extra bucks at market.

Animal cruelty and lessons in business aside, I have a feeling my father also knew the task of sledge hammering the tusks from these poor boars and hanging them from their hind feet to slice into their bodies would be madness. He had to have known that packing a pound of salt in each vacant testicular cavity would elicit the wildest of reactions from these creatures. He had to have known there was a distinct possibility something terrible would happen. My father thrives when the stakes are high. He appreciates drama more than he lets on and I have long suspected he goes looking for it to satisfy a quota known only to him.

Now, I will credit my father with being a brave, if unconventional, lead in this particular tale, but there is something that must be noted. Doug Hoult made it possible. Doug Hoult invited chaos into his life and on to his farm, he let things spiral out of control—the hogs ate and ate until they were too big for him to handle. He was a fool, some might say, but there are others (me?) who might call him a catalyst too: a speck of dust upon which the entire story crystalizes. Was it Doug Hoult who brought this story into being so that my father might play the lead role?

I think I know what my father would say to this logic. Being an ignoramus doesn't make you a catalyst for anything but trouble. Being lazy is inefficient and usually brings unnecessary harm to someone (or, in the case of Hoult, some pigs). Of course, he's right. And while I appreciate my father's intent to demonstrate the value of careful management, I am simultaneously horrified by the sequence of events instigated by Hoult's negligence. I don't condone his actions, or for that matter, my father's.

In the end, the whole incident didn't leave Hoult any better off than he'd started. One of the boars succumbed to infection and though the second fetched a better price at market, he'd made no more money than if he'd left those poor creatures alone.

Tyler and I reluctantly put ourselves to the task of shoving one dank and fetid body after another into my two-door Honda, hoping the newspaper I'd thrown down earlier would be enough to soak up any moisture. (For the record, it wasn't.) The "mother" of the pair, a greying bulge with four black limbs that kicked at irregular intervals, was irascible beyond reason. In an attempt to illustrate her displeasure, she removed a sizeable piece of foam from the passenger seat when the opportunity to do so presented itself. Her daughter was darker, slightly less tousled, and far more aggressive. As we wrangled them, the girl tried half-heartedly—after all, we'd already paid in full—to assuage our budding apprehension. The trauma of changing owners was like a late-in-life adoption, she offered. We needed to give them time to adjust. With a little hand-feeding and soft-talk, we'd be on our way.

As we drove off, the girl mentioned in the most casual way possible, that the goats *might* be pregnant.

A two-hour drive hadn't seemed important on the way out, but the return trip was excruciating. The goats bleated angrily the entire time, and relieved themselves on multiple occasions.

123

I could spend the next fifty pages explaining all of the things that went wrong with these goats during their tenure in our makeshift pen. In summary, they hated me, and so were not willing to be milked, sheered, or coddled in any way. Their fur was disgusting; their attitudes were worse. Even so, my husband, though quite surprised and far less affected by the whimsical imaginings of what raising goats could be, was supportive of our new hobby.

We kept the goats for several years, during which time, they both did give birth. We tried to indoctrinate the kids with our kind words and affection, but herd mentality conquered and despite our best efforts it deteriorated into an "us against them" situation. Eventually, we gave our four goats away to a family down the street who needed some blackberry bushes cleared.

There are dozens of poor decisions that shaped the story I have just recounted. I can list a few, to prove I am not blind to my own process:

1. No research on which goats can be milked
2. No appropriate method for transporting goats
3. General lack of knowledge regarding all goat activities/needs
4. Buying goats that hate people

5. Buying goats that can escape an electrified enclosure with ease
6. Confusing idyllic visions of animal husbandry with the reality of animal care

Obviously, I could go on. The whole experience was a disaster and a substantial draw on our financial and emotional resources. When I told my father we'd given the goats away, he was disappointed. Why on earth had we raised them, if not to make a profit in some way? I didn't say so at the time, but monetary profit seemed an insufficient means of measurement. We didn't make money, or wool, or cheese, but we learned some valuable lessons, namely that we have no interest in raising goats. Pigs though, I wonder if we might enjoy raising pigs.

Despite the hassle, I recall the goat-years with intense fondness. We kept them until our first boy was born and it was time to move east to be closer to family. But since moving back to Maine, the number of times I have belly laughed at the hell those animals put us through easily falls in the hundreds. I can still picture my husband, his lanky body being dragged through mud and muck, arms extended, fingers tangled in the thick matted haunch wool of poor Ninny Muggins as she ran terrified through the pen. I can see the panicky eyes of Lolo as her belly contracted with the pressure of twins. I feel the freshly dried wool of a tiny body in my hands, smell the musk of damp straw and sweet grain, and marvel at the newness of a life.

The Palermo farm.

The Long Winter

The baby has croup again.

I'm standing outside the back door of our new farm in the arctic night. Starlight shimmers at the crest of each icy ridge, making our snow-covered yard feel somehow colder. The cold is why I'm here. The baby's little airways are struggling to draw breath, a wheezing dangerous cough echoes in the darkness. But I know his breathing will soon slow, his airways, iced with each inhale, will shrink, will allow him to drift back into a peaceful sleep. But until then, I am standing here in my long underwear, thinking, shivering.

He is our third baby. The one we'll eventually spoil because we're so tired of trying to control the first two. But control isn't the right word, not really. This family is an exercise in entropic decay—each day an unraveling and manifest proof of the second law of thermodynamics. But as the weeks and years stack up we're also moving forward. The oldest sometimes reads books to his sister as she lies quietly on the couch. The middle tells jokes and dances wild to make the baby laugh. These are people, testing the world with their hearts first, being broken and remade before our very eyes.

I am tired. My feet are bare within these boots. There wasn't time for socks as I shuffled through the bedroom and down the hall, trying to let the others sleep while the baby cried and coughed. There's never time for socks. What a strange thing to equate with luxury. I used to love bare feet, even in the dead of winter on a cold tile kitchen floor. As a child I remember vividly my mother's near constant obsession with keeping my feet warm in winter. The Freedom Farm was always cold. Upstairs toilet bowls crusted with ice and a furnace set to prevent pipes from freezing and little else. I remember playing on the kitchen floor until the soles of my feet burned with cold, ached and tingled. I would lie beneath the cook stove and place my calloused heels upon the cast iron to feel another kind of burn. I had no interest in the luxury of a sock. There was something about that farm, or was it our parents, that pushed us to prove our toughness in whatever way we could. And while I'm slightly embarrassed to admit my own current craving for a warm pair of woolen socks, I am secretly pleased that my children reject my own motherly urging in this arena.

This house protests this shift to sub zero too, she growls deep, foundation adjusting to unseen forces. I find that I am annoyed by her input. We're not on good terms.

It is our second winter in this post and beam

from the late 1850s and my nostalgia has made way for animosity. This is an old house. I can see the basement light through the living room floor. It is a constant reminder that almost nothing stands between the unsavory residents of that space and the ones up here. When the furnace kicks on, the smell of dank soil and stale tobacco pushes through the vents, a century's old sensorial assault.

Before we signed the papers, my parents warned us about old houses. They tried to make us understand that they come with so much more than quaint window trim and soapstone sinks. There is always a wealth of unseen misery. I knew it was true. I'd lived it. Our old bean farm and her frozen pipes, bats in the kitchen, cracking foundation, water in the basement, and cold. So cold. But when we walked through this house, when I saw the cast iron cook stove, its shiny chrome bumpers and warming oven were an invitation filled with sweet nostalgia. We would take the bad with the good we said. We would build memories in this beautiful place.

But houses like these—they have memories of their own.

We don't know much about the people who lived here before us. What we do know comes from neighborhood whispers and a mixture of conjecture and circumstantial evidence. Medicine cabinet knobs so worn with use that a secondary ring, a tiny wooden moat, strangely smooth, circles the round knob. At first, I didn't know what it might mean. I reached a hand to open the cabinet door for cleaning, felt my palm rest easy upon the knob. My fingers lightly grasped to pull, and they slipped gently to the circle of bare wood, white paint long lost to the hands that came before mine. Was it me, or the house itself, that stood accusing those hands of something more sinister? Hands so ravenous for this cabinet's contents their outstretched digits rubbed wood to dust.

And what darkness does it spell that the attic held black and white images of children, swaddled and forever quiet. Memories so painful they were left behind. Should we have kept these pictures? Should we have claimed the sadness that someone else could no longer bear? This house has been home before. It has seen the darkest corners of a human heart. Grief has dragged itself through the hallways, a nightmarish ghoul, desperate and dangerous.

Joy has been here too. Already, we can attest to that. Our youngest boy was born within these walls. A first breath was drawn here. A family grew. Certainly there was joy before us. Yet joy seems impossible to detect without memory. What physical evidence do we leave behind when our hearts are light? Without the memory of dance parties and children playing, scuff marks, dirty walls, and broken windows are merely a list of items to fix, jobs to be done.

This old house is her own memory box and while I know it is fantastical thinking, I can't help but feel that our current disconnect stems from a mutual lack of trust.

Practical people have realistic timelines. They make sure they know exactly what they're getting into, and so, make fewer mistakes. Practical people take calculated risks to maximize possible reward. They take stock of a situation and when it comes to work, they do it once. I am not a practical person. I do none of these things with regularity. In fact, I enjoy the uncalculated risk. It's an absolutely foolish way to approach life.

That's how we ended up in this house, on these 43 acres, within spitting distance of the old Freedom Farm.

When the paperwork was finished, when we'd signed ourselves into considerable debt, my husband noticed that the name on the mortgage didn't match his legal name. Much to his amusement, he proclaimed himself exempt from the financial responsibility of this venture. I'll never know if the timing of his realization was a deliberate step back or a happy coincidence, as he claims.

• • •

The barn, a bonus structure, which came with our new old house, is a massive building with almost no discernable value or purpose. It is unmistakably about to collapse. During much of the first summer, my husband could be found crouched beneath the unsupported floor beams, digging giant holes through the mud to plant stabilizing sonotubes. At this same time, I moved from room to room with a paint roller in hand, in a vain attempt to eliminate the odor of cats. Our three small children were quarantined to the downstairs living space for fear they'd discover the sweet taste of lead paint chips.

The barn wasn't our only structural concern. The fieldstones stacked beneath the workshop and woodshed had been haphazardly removed to "improve the aesthetic" of the place. These unsightly stones had served as the foundation to these buildings for a century. This information was passed to us with casual disinterest by the previous homeowner, who was now completely untethered to the consequences of his own ignorance. If it weren't so dire a situation, we might have laughed. Removing the stones had a secondary benefit, the old man assured us. It created a neat space beneath the buildings for storage. Storage of what, I am uncertain, as the space was no higher than a knee. Even if we'd wanted to slide a couple of garden implements beneath these crooked sills, the storage space was infested with weasels.

As I stand here in the dark, watching my baby's chest rise and fall with ease, I am struck by the beauty of the night. The stars are so bright out here, in the country. They are a comfort. They remind me of my mother, her arms wrapped tightly around me as we lay in the driveway of the Freedom Farm, covered in blankets, searching for the next meteor. Bright. Quiet. Peaceful. Last winter, while the two smaller babies slept, I crept to my oldest boy's side and shook him awake. We found blankets and hats on our way to the front steps. We sat together in silence, looking up, waiting for a streak of light to surprise us. My arms held his tiny body, my heart filled with a memory turned inside out.

There are so many rats.

One might think that in a house, riddled with claw marks and dried puddles of cat dominance, that the rodent population would be negligible. Yet, the rats are so abundant they have begun the work of domesticating themselves. They are so free from Darwinian pressures that the majority of their time is spent on personal maintenance, social dalliances, and occasional afternoon sunbathing sessions beneath the bird feeder. Their brown and white patches scream privilege and abundance. These are not creatures fighting the harsh realities of nature. They are well-groomed members of an organized colony. They are a team of sophisticated terrorists.

We borrowed a small gun from my father and began hunting by daylight. Rats are nocturnal but there were so many on the property they'd taken to hunting in shifts. Day shift was for the smaller rats, the ones working their way up the corporate ladder. The kill count was recorded on our whiteboard. This amused my father, so in his spare time, he'd come over and set up a chair in the living room, open our window, and wait, gun raised, for one to run by. It was almost too easy to pick them off. Almost.

It didn't seem to matter how many day rats were eliminated. More came. We could hear them in the walls, ceilings, scurrying in the barn whenever the door was opened.

Then, this fall, as the weather turned colder, the rats started dying. We began finding rat carcasses on the driveway, in the yard, on our front steps. Perhaps there was no longer enough food. Perhaps they turned on one another. Spring will bring answers.

Or spring will bring rats.

There are snowy owls in these woods. Just the other day I saw one overhead as the baby and I walked in the cold air together. We both needed to get out of the house—to fill our chests with an icy reminder to breathe. Life feels hard when the days are short and the wind blows too cold. Bodies are slow to move, slow to feel anything at all.

I told my daughter, just three, about the owl. Her eyes went wide, her body still. Having read *Owl Moon* by Jane Yolen dozens of times, I could see she was wondering beyond imagination, into story. For her, the story was a little girl and her mother in the snow. They walked beneath the moon, bundled heavy to ward the wind and ice. Together they crept, step by step, deeper into the night. Owling. Searching the skies for the moon shadow cast by wide wings.

She begged to go with me, to live the story, feel the cold on her face, the wind in her ears. This child pushed against the inertia of Maine winter, she shifted us both beyond the warmth of the fire and into the woods. I carried her, wrapped tight against my body, into the forest. We walked for miles, the snow giving way to my weight in fits and bursts. Her eyes scoured the treetops for signs while mine kept us clear of sticks and rocks buried just beneath the surface of the snow. Eventually her eyelids grew heavy, her head fell against my chest. Instead of bringing her home to rest, I kept walking. I fell into a rhythmic memory, each step deeper into the land that was now mine. Each step an echo of the journeys I'd taken as a child through gullies and cedar forests, beneath pine boughs drooping with heavy snow, behind the Freedom Farm. This is the way land becomes a part of you, if you let it.

I've been looking at new houses, ones with more bedrooms and less problems. A house near the city might be nice. We could go out more. I want a house with kitchen floors that are level, new windows, heat pumps, and insulation. I want a house with office space, a new roof, a garage to park in. I know homes like this exist. We could sell this place and buy one.

But . . .

Would there be owls? Would there be such pure starlight and acres of snow-covered fields? Would winter feel like a battle hard fought?

There are people, amphiscians, who because of their latitude, have noon shadows that fall to both sides, dependent on the season. This image, of shadow to both sides, will not let go of me. A middle ground, a ground that does not move but nonetheless, is two things at once. I am struggling to find the place where my own shadow should fall. At a crossroads to a future I cannot yet picture in either direction. Am I made for old houses, cold nights and woolen socks to battle icy floors? Or am I suited for something more modern?

• • •

I consider this place a farm. It is sentimentality, mostly, but an assertion that can be justified with ease. For a property to qualify as a farm it must satisfy only one condition. A farm, by definition is land upon which an industrial function is carried out. Industry: a productive enterprise. Enterprise: a project.

Is family not a worthy project? Are the people on this farm not growing, learning, and evolving? Whether these things are productive is another matter, but I'd be willing to place a bet.

The baby and I are ready to go inside. My body is cold to the bones and his is settled into the rhythm of deep sleep. His name means "Valley of Oaks," and as I look to the distant boundary of our hillside, I am reminded of that synchronicity. This property has some of the most majestic oak trees I've ever seen. They are everywhere, making shade for the kids as they roll in the grass, dig for worms, and hang from branches.

I think we'll wait out this long winter together—all of us. We'll plant a garden this spring with snap peas, potatoes, zucchini, and carrots. I'll do the weeding. The kids will over-water. And I have no doubt that the house will stand here, collecting evidence, in the way that houses do.

Who knows, maybe we'll stay.

Citizen's Arrest

In this flow, mind and matter are not separate substances. Rather, they are different aspects of our whole and unbroken movement.

—David Bohm,
Wholeness and the Implicate Order

I'm going to write something that isn't true yet. It's not fiction. Fiction implies falsehood or fantasy and that's not what I'm talking about. What I'm going to write might be true. Let's call it: Speculative Nonfiction. But first—

Quite by accident I stumbled upon the work of the late David Bohm. He was a theoretical physicist who spent a great deal of time and energy trying to describe both mathematically and philosophically that separateness is an illusion. Rather—this is my unscientific and simplistic distillation of his theories. Another way to put it might be: We (each of us) are both a part of and the entirety of the whole. In this case, "the whole" means everything, all of what we see, feel, experience, think, and create. Our collective perception of reality is a product of our collective projections of that reality.

What does this mean on a practical level?

I don't really know. Maybe Bohm's way of thinking would eliminate our ability to separate ourselves from the suffering of others. Or perhaps it would empower those who might otherwise feel powerless to positively impact the world in which they live.

While these are lofty and worthy goals, what drew me to Bohm's work was more personal. It was a phrase in an article I can no longer find, or at least, I think it was. The article was meant as a rudimentary introduction to a number of prevailing quantum-mechanical theories. In the section about Bohm's work, the author explained that, according to Bohm, we are all projections of ourselves.

It was the word projection; the idea that I could be both a present and a future version of myself, a self thrust forward through time, a not-yet-self.

I'm new to writing Speculative Nonfiction, but it seems the tense to use would be first person present. This is the tense of imagining.

I am sitting on a bench. The wood slats are a little damp, but I'm wearing an old pair of jeans, so it doesn't really bother me. Or maybe I'm just standing near the bench, thankful I didn't sit down before inspecting it. (Have I just switched into speculative first person present?)

The bench and I are in a city park, sometime between noon and 3 p.m. I don't know the exact time, but that's not really important. The important thing is that most people are plodding away at their 9-5 jobs while I'm in the park with the retirees. The sun is shining and I hear birds chirping from nearby trees. There is one chipmunk that won't quit chattering and it has just struck me that I might be in his territory.

Off to my left, beneath the canopy of a few large-leaf maples there is an elderly man out for a stroll. He's carrying something but I can't quite make it out. Maybe it's a cane or a stick he's found blocking the path. I can tell by the way his glance is tracing the trail ahead that he will choose the route leading to me. I am not particularly interested in our inevitable interaction.

Before I go on, I think this is important:

Recently, a friend of mine got into some trouble. I'm usually not one to qualify friend-ships, but in this particular case, I feel it might be important to mention that the nature of our relationship was closer to: chummy feelings towards an acquaintance with underlying and not immediately obvious psychologically question-able behaviors. In any case, this friend casually mentioned that we might need to work together to "get our story straight" in the event we were brought before a judge. To be clear, there was no "our story" because at the time this friend was getting into her predicament, I was at home sleeping.

I'm not one to brush off nonchalance in the face of the law. I immediately addressed the misconception that I was in any way the kind of person who would lie to a judge. In fact, I instructed my friend to cease and desist any sharing of information she would not want reported verbatim to anyone wearing a uniform. I can't remember if I told her I would confess to a postal worker if asked directly, but if I didn't, I should have.

I am the kind of person who, in almost all circumstances, does not/cannot lie. Once in a while I eat cherries from the bag before I've paid for it in the grocery store. It's not that I don't see the utility of being capable of a lie. I do. I sometimes wish I could handle a small one here and there. But when tasked with lying, I am an exaggerated version of the worst liars on every television crime drama you've ever seen. Sure, I get sweaty palms and my eyes dart around the room, but it isn't just the common physical manifestations of the lie that give me away. I get unmistakably weird. I make bizarre and embarrassing noises. It's almost as though my vocal chords take it upon themselves to physically rebel against untruth.

Obviously, putting me before a judge to corroborate a "story" would be a horrible blunder for any criminal. Yet this is not the reason I refused to do so. I have scruples. I, more than anyone I know, appreciate rules. No. Appreciate seems too lukewarm. It's possible to *appreciate* a good night's rest. I am passionately protective of rules and the individuals/communities they safeguard.

Some people are contrary by nature, irritated by societal shackles and burdened by the weight of regulation. I am not one of those people. I go the speed limit with pleasure, wait in lines, and pay taxes without complaint. Graffiti personally offends me no matter how artistically pure the vandal's intentions were. I enjoy paperwork because it makes me feel organized, prepared, and productive. I respect rules. For the most part, I believe in the organizing bodies that create them. Naturally, I find it distasteful when others consider themselves above the law. I admire the work of those who try to improve upon existing systems, but I do not feel that personal preference gives anyone the right to exist outside of their current bounds.

It should not come as a surprise then, that prior to my departure from this world, there is one action, which, if the conditions are right and I am given the opportunity, I will take without hesitation: a citizen's arrest.

I've been talking about this for years. It's become the thing I mention at parties to get the conversation moving. Sometimes partygoers are caught up in the details. How will I detain this person? Do I travel with handcuffs? Is this actually legal? Once in a while a stranger will give me a head to toe scan and inform me that the individual I arrest will have to be on their deathbed. Though somewhat hurt by the insinuation that I am incapable of taking down a more robust offender, this insult is not far from the mark. I am not a large person. Nor am I a particularly bold one. I possess what I believe to be an appropriately high level of paranoia in regard to the possibility that a criminal may seek revenge for their notice/capture.

I've started walking toward the old man now, tired of hearing the chipmunk's high-pitched ranting, ready to get on with my day. The man is close enough that I can see he is holding an umbrella. That makes sense. It's Washington. The rain comes and goes with little warning. Or maybe it's a paper bag. Or binoculars.

Here's where things get hazy. The old man thinks he sees someone from his past, a woman, across the street in the café opposite the park. He darts across the road faster than I thought he could move. There's no crosswalk. He's almost hit by several cars, whose drivers have to slam on their brakes and swerve.

Or maybe he doesn't cross the road. Maybe he sits down on a bench similar to the one I thought about sitting on and pulls a flask from his paper bag. Maybe I watch while he gulps down a liter of Captain Morgan's then takes off his clothes to enjoy the sun on his naked flesh.

Maybe he ignores a series of "No Trespassing" signs along the perimeter of the park and wanders onto private property.

No matter what he does, I'm paying attention. I notice he has committed a misdemeanor.

One question might be: do I even know what qualifies as a misdemeanor? And since this scenario takes place in the future, I think it's fair to leave it at: I *will* know. Right now I'm satisfied with the knowledge that the definition of misdemeanor could change depending on the jurisdiction.

Another question might be: Do I really believe myself capable of arresting someone? I'd like to. I'd like to believe that I'm the kind of person who is willing to enforce our society's rules without fear of retribution, a person who cannot be coerced into inaction or ambivalence. The citizen's arrest is a beautiful merger of personal justice and democracy. In what other way can one be both a vigilante and a lover of the law? My desire to perform one says: I am unafraid. I am powerful. I am willing to do what is right not just for myself, but also for the common good.

It is my not-yet-self that performs a citizen's

arrest. She is a projection, a mantra, a wish to be more than I am.

I have tried imagining hundreds of scenarios in which I complete my arrest and there has only been one, Elderly Man in Park (with minor variations), which passes as remotely possible. The arrest always transpires with unprecedented cordiality.

Having witnessed the crime, I approach and kindly inform the man of his indiscretion. He wrings his hands, apologizes profusely and finds it difficult to look me in the eye. In the spirit of full disclosure, I explain that it has been my lifelong dream to citizen's arrest someone and he agrees that this is the perfect opportunity. We make our way to the police station, which happens to be within walking distance, to fill out the paperwork. Maybe we stop for coffee along the way.

In the end, justice is served and the old man and I become pen pals while he spends a few weeks in a minimum-security facility. Or maybe he just does community service for a few months. I don't even know the penalty for a misdemeanor.

Considering I am incapable of imagining an arrest that does not involve a repentant octogenarian, it seems that I have some grasp of my own limitations. Yet, I know myself well enough to admit that I will continue to proclaim my intentions with the same bravado and vagueness as always. Not because I feel the need to inflate my own importance, well, maybe a little of that, but mostly because I believe holding fast to the citizen's arrest is actually helping to reinforce the ideals it represents. The how and when of my not-yet-arrest is far less important than the why.

If I am a projection of myself, if I am allowed to push forward through time a version of me that is better, more capable, fearless, and willing to make this world safer one elderly lawbreaker at a time, why wouldn't I? Projecting values is like creating a future-self to keep me accountable. This is my version of Bohm's unbroken movement, an attempt to live not just in the moment, but toward something more than I am right now.

Tulip Petunia

February 18, 2019

This year, winter has been more difficult than expected. February, in particular, is stretching beyond what seems a reasonable duration. A snowstorm is expected on Sunday, and though the forecasters would have us believing it'll be worthy of a name, the general public seems to have caught on that this tactic is a ploy to create some excitement where none duly resides. Winter storm Henry or Ida or Kip, it really doesn't matter to the Mainer, whose primary concern is keeping a woodstove stoked until the weather turns.

There has been one unfortunate source of excitement on our little farm. Today there was a beaver on the premises. I wish it were better circumstances, for the beaver, but it seems our dog Tulip has either hunted this creature, or found it already dispatched and carried it home. The first scenario seems unlikely, as Tulip has no concept of the appropriate distance from which to launch an attack. She has been observed stalking a squirrel from 200 yards away. At 195 yards she pounces mightily and scares the creature into hiding well in advance of her enthusiastic approach.

There are some who love their dogs like they

love their people. This indiscriminate affection has long perplexed me. Dogs are not people. While I could spend pages examining the minutia of these two species differences, I think it might suffice to keep it simple. Dogs will eat dirty diapers until they are hospitalized. Then, they will do it again the next day, if given the opportunity. This is not a direct attack on the intelligence of dogs. It is an observation of the power of instinct, the distance these animals are from their initial domestication, and the impossibility of shifting their behavior to something more civilized. Dogs are essentially nice coyotes.

Despite knowing this, I believed our family needed a dog. When my youngest child was just three weeks old, we welcomed Tulip Petunia into our home. She was the tiniest pup. Even though all the books I'd read indicated that a puppy should approach strangers with a wagging tail and unbridled exuberance, I chalked it up to a tender heart when Tulip did not act in this way. She needed a little more coddling. A new mother of three, I was sensitive to the needs of a puppy. I often compared the dog's behavior to that of my infant. She was needy, but understandably so. This ball of brown fur had been taken from her mother, a thought that broke my heart and blinded me to the truth.

But I digress. Let's get back to the beaver, which was clearly a juvenile, something that

Tulip took no pains to hide from my own juvenile as she chewed this poor creature next to a half-constructed snowman in the front yard. Our son, who came running into the house screaming about a pool of blood and a floppy carcass, alerted us to the beaver's presence. The appalling image of Tulip with her play-thing had not, for better or worse, traumatized the boy, but it did seem prudent to resolve the situation before his younger sister caught wind of things.

I am employed part time with a company that, for reasons beyond my belief, agrees to let me choose my hours, work from home, and disappear for days on end when things get busy at home. This work situation is both ideal and incredibly inconvenient when searching for reasons to avoid unpleasant tasks associated with raising children, dogs, and dealing with various other farm-related chores. My flexibility made it impossible to defer the task of separating a dog from a beaver and hiding said beaver far, far away. I trudged across the road and back toward the pond, holding the limp creature high above the snow so as not to create a scent trail for the dog to follow. When I'd gone a good distance, I flung the thing into a thicket and turned to be on my way.

Back at the house, Tulip was running frenzied circles in the kitchen. She'd been separated from her conquest long enough and was determined to get back to it. Fairly certain I'd handled the situation, I released Tulip to the wild and returned to my desk to continue working. Not twenty minutes later, the boy was screaming from the living room window that the beaver was back.

The second beaver removal fell to my husband. He must have done a similar walk into the woods, because an hour more and the beaver was spotted a third time, now in the back yard. At this point we realized it had become an elaborate and rather distasteful game of hide and seek for Tulip Petunia, who happened to be enjoying herself immensely. It was increasingly difficult to tolerate her jubilance as she retrieved this now ghastly beaver from truly astonishing locations.

Finally, we determined that the only safe place was the top of our compost hut—a seven-foot jump. We would deal with a more permanent solution when we weren't so involved in our work. The beaver did not reappear.

Tomorrow we will get our girl cleaned up. Nails trimmed, hair cut, body thoroughly washed of beaver blood and the musty dampness that accompanies dogs who endure the constant shift from dry to wet to dry again during a long Maine winter.

February 19, 2019

Tulip is a big fluffy ball of brown fur, a frantic poof of a creature, spreading the fragrance of lavender soap throughout the house. On grooming days she seems to understand that love flows more freely, we all pet her more frequently and play games with her in the kitchen as she jauntily trots about from person to person.

Before getting Tulip, I read books on proper training techniques. I was diligent about socializing our puppy early and with great frequency. I knew it was important to have her meet and play with men and children, to familiarize her with the process of meeting and greeting as many people as possible. I read about positive reinforcement, about creating good behavior with consistent rewards.

Our friends and family thought we were crazy to get a puppy with an infant in the house, but it was actually strategically planned. I was nursing a baby anywhere from two to one hundred times a night, so whenever I got up to nurse, I brought Tulip outside for a quick training session. It was winter, so the trips weren't always pleasant, but it worked. She was house trained quickly and seemed genuinely delighted with the arrangement. We were in a sweet spot. It was before Tulip's many character flaws began to intersect with a multitude of my own preconceived notions about how a dog should behave.

Tulip didn't have a middle name at first. It was just Tulip. But as things progressed and my need to adequately express my frustration increased, I really needed that middle name to distinguish different levels of my own emotional distress.

February 20, 2019
The beaver is back.

It is incomprehensible to me how Tulip has managed to dislodge the beaver from a location well above my own head. But she did. Nathan has become so peeved by the constant disruptions to his workday that he has decided there is only one more option. We have to throw the beaver away. We have to bag it like common household garbage and put it in a garbage can in the closed garage.

Why does this feel so inappropriate?

The problem is that Tulip is too complicated. She is a mix between a lab and a poodle. This seemed the perfect combination to me. Labs, while usually somewhat dopey, by reputation are the friendliest, most loving and trusting dogs. I thought that adding some dopiness and blind trust to a paranoia-stricken ball of energy might somehow slow it down and help minimize the needless anxiety. Instead, we found ourselves living with a dog that is very intelligent, but crippled by her own cognitive dissonance. I realize it might make me unpopular to honestly discuss my feelings about one particular dog breed above others, but I'm willing to risk it. Poodles: I've known a couple of poodles, socialized in their circles, and while I think it's bad form to generalize about an entire group of individuals having met only a few, they were noticeably—how should I say this—"off." Don't get me wrong, they're lovely creatures, unique. But if you are hoping that some other breed in a designer match will supersede a poodle's idiosyncrasies, you are mistaken. The strangeness factor of the poodle cannot be suppressed.

Tulip Petunia is a poodle.

February 27, 2019

There are two beavers in my car.

Both creatures are wrapped in the flimsy white plastic of generic kitchen garbage bags. I meant to dispose of them about a week ago, but when I'd finished loading the car with heaps of garbage and recycling, I discovered, quite unhappily, that the transfer station was closed. Time got away from me and it is just now, today, that I remember the car has been slowly absorbing the unpleasant odors of household refuse and expired pond residents for six full days.

You might be wondering how one beaver became two.

So am I.

The second beaver appeared a few days after the first. We bagged it immediately. We're all just hoping we've reached the end of this ordeal.

• • •

April 05, 2019

Today I spotted a wild turkey about three hundred yards from the back door. We own about forty-three acres, ample space for our own children and local wildlife to comingle and explore. The property winds back in a series of connected fields with several small copses and large oaks dotting the open areas. The turkey was heading into the back field, almost out of sight when I opened the door to let Tulip out. Jokingly, I told her to "go get it."

I got back to dishes and cleaning and was as shocked as the rest of the family when an hour later my son was screaming at the back door that Tulip had another dead animal. Everyone ran to see what she'd found this time—all of us believing wholeheartedly that the beavers had died of cold and lack of food at the tail end of a long winter—not as a result of our girl Tulip.

She was carrying that damned turkey toward me like she was delivering a briefcase full of money. Her eyes were shining with pride and while my heart sank at the realization that we'd never be able to raise chickens, I had to give her a pat and tell her she was a good girl. She'd done exactly what I asked.

I do my best to love this dog like a dog: without qualification, prerequisites, or boundaries. I fail daily. For this reason, I am glad that dogs are not people. Tulip Petunia does not hold grudges. She wags her tail and follows me around until I grab her and pet her and tell her she's a good girl no matter how many diapers she eats or how many beavers I have to cart to the dump.

Tulip Petunia taking a rest.

Rocks, Rocking, and Ricochets

When we moved into our new old house two summers ago, there was an abandoned well just outside our back door. It was covered with a cement block and some wire mesh, and served as an eyesore the year round. Over coffee one morning in early spring, I decided I wanted a patio instead of a cement block covering a giant hole. I'd never built a patio, but two YouTube videos later I felt confident it was a matter of labor, not skill to get the project done. This is how many projects arise in our home.

From nothingness—while I drink my coffee.

Nathan wasn't noticeably opposed to the idea, so I ran with it. The first step in creating a patio is leveling the surface. Normally people use a shovel to remove high spots, maybe dig in a couple of inches, and then use a rake to flatten. I started by opening up the well cover and undoing what must have been hundreds of hours of labor. There was something both satisfying and deeply disturbing about dismantling and then filling a well that had served our house's residents for almost two hundred years. I spent the better part of a day throwing shovelful after shovelful of earth back into the hole. We never did measure the depth, but it must have been almost six feet in diameter. While digging and filling, I decided to remove the top two or three layers of flat stones from the structure of the well to use for landscaping. These stones were hundreds, in some cases, upward of a thousand pounds and had probably been pulled by horses or cattle to be laid within the well ring. I insisted that my husband drag these stones with his tractor to the top of a hill behind our house so that I could create a stone staircase. Since moving in, I have imagined a whimsical hillside garden, embellished with a stone staircase, flowers, and a mulberry tree (which incidentally has been planted, but refuses to grow).

While the patio construction and my numerous missteps while completing it might be of interest to some, it is both embarrassing and irrelevant to this story, which follows the stones. Nathan and I talked about renting an excavator to lift and place these rocks, or using our own tractor to roll them with logs and levers. But as often happens, I became restless, impatient. The stones were killing the grass at the top of the hill, leaving brown scars in my well-tended lawn. Something had to be done *now*.

It took almost an hour to move the first stone about seven inches. First, I had to find the perfect birch rounds for rolling. Our log piles were full of soft pine, a few oak logs, and every here and

Digging the patio.

there, a perfectly circular, sixteen-inch birch. It seemed a shame to use such a beautiful log for this grunt work, but nevertheless I selected about five rounds with diameters between three and six inches, and then found a nice flat rock to brace my crowbar against as I worked. Materials collected, it was time to begin lifting, shifting, propping, and rolling. This kind of movement did not come naturally for me. Putting all of my weight on the crowbar would lift the stone ever so slightly, just enough to prop one side so that I could shift my wedge to the other. The motions were often counterintuitive; pulling the crowbar back would shift the stone forward. Pushing the crowbar down and forward would wiggle the stone back. As I learned to maneuver the lever, to predict the most effort-efficient way to wiggle the stone, it began to move more quickly.

Finally, the first of the giants sat crooked at the very apex of the hill, threatening to slide downward. I prepared a spot for it about ten feet below, flattening the earth, packing it down. From where the stone sat to about three feet above where I wanted it, I placed birch rounds. These were meant to act as aids to keep the rock moving just fast enough to land in place and stop.

It was at this moment that Nathan walked out the back door for his lunch break. It is unclear whether he was just thrilled at the prospect of taking part in the final shove or horrified that I might flatten myself unintentionally. In any case, he came running.

Becoming parents is also a transition from potential to kinetic energy, a setting loose of intention with limited ability to guide outcome. So far, our children have shown themselves to be stubborn, determined, and undeterred by the constraints of reality. Nathan and I agree that all of their personality flaws must have skipped a generation with us, and their positive traits are a direct result of our superb parenting skills. While we would have hoped that our influence be a bit longer-lasting, we have discovered that at six, three, and one, they have already proven that the safest thing for Nathan and I to do is to get out of their way.

I toggle between feelings of awe and horror at the grandness of the task before us. These are people, complicated, driven, beautiful, both strong and delicate. These hearts will break with hurt and swell with joy. These bodies will reach for connection. I am left to hope that no matter where they go, they will always know home. It is home that I am trying to build. Whimsical staircases, flowers, forest paths. But, of course, it is more than that. Home is not really a place. It is a collection of stories that tie us together and helps us remember who we are.

From the time my kids were able to wrap their digits around an object and then open them again, they have loved rocks. Rocks for throwing, rocks for collecting, rocks for moving, rocks for friends. The boys do more throwing than anything else, intuitively discovering how an arm can best fling, flip, and skip a stone. The number of times I have insisted one of my boys stop throwing rocks in a public place is impossible to calculate, but the number of windows shattered by flying objects is extremely calculable. If I remember correctly, my eldest first began doing chores and receiving an allowance so that he could pay off the debt he'd incurred as a result of a broken window.

Ogden, the baby of the family, has picked up right where his older brother left off. He loves throwing rocks at houses, other children, and dogs. But perhaps his favorite thing to do is deposit small piles of stones all over the lawn. Of course, as an eighteen-month-old, he isn't fully aware of the consequences of this activity. Lawn mowing has become a high stakes game of hide-and-seek—any missed piles become mini stockpiles of munitions. When hit, they are flung at high speed from the mower's blower and put all who come near in great personal danger.

Nathan likes to play a game with small stones he finds at the pond's edge. He takes one and throws it high into the air. Then, as quickly as he can, he takes aim with the second stone and tries to knock the first off course while it still hangs in the sky. If you have never tried this, I highly recommend it so that you can feel how unbelievably difficult a task this really is. I have never hit my first stone with my second. Nathan does it regularly. As a child, he practiced this game for hours, absorbing the laws of motion, gravity, acceleration—they were becoming a part of him. Now, he can hold two rocks in his hands and he can intuit how they will move through space and time. He has the patience to practice for hours at a simple task when mastery might move him toward understanding something more complex. I wish his patience would extend to farm-related manual labor, but he'd argue that there is no greater lesson to be learned by digging holes for planting apple trees, or weeding strawberry patches. Despite this lack of enthusiasm for run-of-the-mill chores, I do love how he appreciates what we can learn from being present with ourselves in nature.

Nathan and I gave the rock a final push, all four of our hands spread along its longest side. It began to move slowly at first, and then it gathered speed as its trajectory shifted downward. This mammoth stone slipped from one birch log to the next as it traversed the hillside, and the thud as its final roller passed beneath the trailing edge came just before the satisfying finale. The well-stone was now a stair-stone. It sat exactly where I'd hoped it would, halfway down the hill. It was the centerpiece of this new path, a hard-earned victory (with the help of gravity).

There were other stones, and even though none were quite so large, they were equally thrilling to put in place. With each step, I could see my own movement through time. For me, this is the nature of physical labor, of working with my hands. Sometimes, I think we all need to see what we are working toward, and maybe too what we are working to hold onto.

• • •

A few weeks ago my twelve-year-old niece came to visit. She lives in the city and hasn't spent much time away from the hustle and bustle of her hometown. She was delighted by the mysteries of our country life, and took every opportunity to experience the same wildness with which our own children live every day. At the lake one afternoon, she picked up a rock the size of a softball, and to my horror, she tossed it into the air without consideration to the laws of physics. It was as though she had never experimented with projectiles before. She was in no way concerned with the position of her hand as it released the sizable rock just above her own head. She seemed genuinely shocked at the object's trajectory. Just as the rock was about to strike her in the face, she dove out of the way. My children stood in absolute shock, unable to process why someone would do something quite so dangerous. Even for them, the feral, rock-flinging, window-breaking crew, the careless toss had seemed completely insane.

We all took a moment to discuss safety. We touched on the importance of "knowing where you're throwing," of practice, of keeping others safe. The truth was, my niece had maybe never thrown a rock into a lake. She had not grown up with the privilege of acres and acres in which to learn the nature of nature.

• • •

My daughter Bellamy is almost four years old. The power and genius of her imagination cannot be overstated. Where some children have imaginary friends, she has an imaginary assistant. It doesn't seem to matter to her in the least, but I am amused that she unconsciously fights the patriarchy by hiring a male assistant. He also happens to be a bumblebee named Fred.

This child will sit beneath an apple tree, staring into the blue sky with wide eyes and a smile on her face. When you ask her what she is doing, she will point to a knot on the tree's trunk and insist that it is a button that begins the puppet show. It is a show that she is currently watching, and could you please be quiet because she can't hear what the puppets are saying.

Bellamy will collect five or six round stones from the property and bathe them, feed them pistachio nuts, read them stories, and put them to bed. They are her friends, her babies, and her colleagues. In speaking with this almost-four-year-old, it's easy to get lost in a world of underage business management. Nature is not something she discovers, it is something she uses to create. Nature is her temp agency, providing a list of qualified assistants that want nothing more than to work for her.

My daughter appreciates the small pieces of white quartz sparkling from beneath the surface of the pond. They are diamonds planted by mermaids. She runs her fingers along the jagged edge of the bluestone in our driveway. If you ask her, she'll tell you that these are called bluestone because if you hold them, your skin turns blue and you transform into an invisible dragon warrior. Her play has no limits when there is earth and stone.

My oldest boy, Jack, is six. Since his fourth birthday he has been working single-mindedly toward a career in herpetology. More specifically, he is passionate about the study and protection of snakes. Would I have preferred he'd taken to something more cuddly and lovable like kittens? Sure. But now that we're on the path, I find I too am captivated by the beauty and versatility of these elusive creatures. Jack takes a practical approach to acquiring knowledge, and has accumulated more snake bites than anyone I know. He has been bitten by no fewer than three species, and astonishingly, continues to seek out interactions with snakes at every possible turn.

"At every turn"—an interesting choice of words for this obsession of his. It is as though the stones on our property have a life of their own, changing position from day to day, hour to hour. "At every turn" I am discovering that rocks I have carefully laid around gardens, walkways and stairs have been carelessly flipped and forgotten. Jack has been informed over and over again that he must cease and desist his destruction of landscaping features, yet he cannot resist the urge to search for a snake. He dismantles stone structures with gusto and complete indifference to his mother's instructions. He does it because "at every turn" of a stone, there is potential. There is a chance he might find what he is looking for. They are only rocks, he says, and he is right, and he is wrong.

Rocks are not only rocks in this family. They are part of all of us, in different ways. They connect this family to what is real, what is right in front of us. They are our conduit of connecting to the moment, to our imaginations and our passions. In a world where kids and adults are being consumed by electronics, our family is consumed by what we can hold in our hands, what we can flip, what we can catch, what we can knock out of the sky.

Throwing rocks at the pond.

Jack and his snakes.

Dear Ezra

Dear Ezra,

The night you were born, I stood half naked in a room full of people who were frozen, stiff with worry, waiting to hear the quiet wheeze of an inhaling breath. They waited—eyes wide, hearts pounding—to know whether your heart would join theirs in the rhythmic pulse of life.

The slate floor must have been cool beneath my bare feet, and I saw the hairs standing straight on my arms and legs but I did not feel them. There is only so much a body can feel. The night you were born was long. It did last and will last for the rest of my life. That's a strange thing to say, I know. You are too young to understand much about time, but I've had thirty-nine years to get a feel for how one moment leads into another and how memories also fade. I've had thirty-nine years to discover that it is exceedingly rare to experience two realities simultaneously, to be in a space where life itself is balanced exactly between not existing at all and existing forever. You, the boy that you will become, hovered in that space with me on the night you were born. We stood together, watching the scene in quiet reverence as the kindness of others shifted the balance toward you.

168

I remember vividly your hands were white. It was my job to hold them. Our midwife was doing the work of saving a life and between breaths told me to rub your tiny hands, to bring sensation to your stillness. Those hands, whose fingers lay slack on the blue couch of our birthing room, I put them into my own and spoke softly to you. Asked you to please stay, to take the air you needed. It could have been a hundred years I knelt beside you, or it could have been ten seconds. Your father held your feet, rubbed the tiny soles with his thumbs, his face showing a worry I could not carry.

You see, I was tired. You did not come easy into the world.

For months I have thought about how best to explain this night to you, how best to explain it to myself. I wondered if there was a way to do so that would help me heal a little from the wound created by the pain I felt that night. But the wound has been healing on its own. Your laugh, the smooth pink skin of your cheeks when you wake from a long sleep, the feel of your fingers wrapped around my own as I rock you. These memories all fold themselves atop the first to give you depth and me distance from that night.

If I close my eyes, I am reliving that scene. I am standing half naked in a room full of people who are frozen, stiff with worry. The birthing pool sits steaming in the corner, empty of the joy it was

169

meant to hold. The windows are open, wanting to welcome a breeze that will not come. Instead, the flashing lights of police and ambulance splash the knotted pine of ceilings and walls. That room has become a room inside me, a place I can go willingly or quite by accident. It is both real and a metaphor for how we move through this world. There is loneliness here. There are places and times when we must live within ourselves to fight our private battles, to find our purpose, to be authentic. The night you were born, I was strong in a way I never had been before. I stood alone within myself holding hope in my heart instead of fear.

Though make no mistake, Ezra, I was never alone. Your father held my hands as I screamed you into existence. His bearded cheek pressed hard into mine, pleading to share the waves of agony as they came. I felt his heart crack open to wrap itself around you. Our midwife held your body with her warm hands. They were steady, strong, capable. Four big men, paramedics and police officers, stood in a line, heads bowed, hands clenched against the unimaginable. They watched in awe as your lungs were inflated over and over again. They covered me in a towel and their goodness filled the room. Your grandmothers paced circles around the kitchen island. They were both calling to you through this world and into the unknown. Calling with prayers so loud and fierce I'm sure you could hear them. I could.

The night you were born was on the first of June and I carry it every day as a reminder of how lucky we all are to know you. Welcome home.

Leaving Time

There is a picture of my mother on her thirtieth birthday. She has long brown-black hair that I know has been straightened. It must have been humid that November because there are signs of frizz, hovering just beyond the outline of her head. She is unmistakably beautiful. She is laughing a laugh I know well because it is hers and it is mine. The skin on her face is smooth and brown and her right eye is a little smaller than her left because, like me, she cannot help squinting when her mouth opens with a smile. Her shirt is burnt orange and ribbed. The neck a slit running from shoulder to shoulder, that is just wide enough to expose the ridges of curved collarbones and the valleys they protect.

That orange shirt was passed to me, eventually. I kept it well into my twenties, as both a reminder of my mother and of the woman in that picture.

Every few years I have an attack. It comes on slowly, a gradual tightening of purpose. Like a dog leaving home in search for a quiet place to let go—I am drawn to my memory of the old Freedom Farm. I am called to a Leaving Time, to a time of breaking apart, moving forward.

My first great loss was the Freedom Farm.

It was the only home I'd ever known and it wasn't my choice to let it go. But, I did let it go. I let it slip from my heart so gently that I sometimes wonder if I ever loved it at all. The day before we left for good, I took pictures in black and white. I wanted to preserve the beauty, but couldn't bring myself to include the color. It was already leaching from the place, soaking through my memories. The lilacs by the barn, petals like tiny purple bruises, transformed to gray scale.

Though my father called them weeds, my mother and I always agreed that milkweed flowers smelled the sweetest. When gone to seed, they'd pepper our fields with nuisance shoots. Even so, she let some grow, hidden beneath the tree across the road, just so I could smell them. Lupine, purple, white, pink, she snuck the browning pods from neighbors' plots to start her own. Lilac hung beside the clothesline, cream and violet.

On my own thirtieth birthday I walked along the Melaka River, through the cobblestones of its old city, my sandaled feet brown and callused. The soles of my cheap shoes melted ever so slightly to the hot stones beneath my feet. But what I remember most are the flowers. Purples, blues, vibrant fuchsia, they hung in baskets by the riverbank and every once in a while I would lean in to smell them.

· · ·

In the photo, my mother sits just right of center, unaware that I will be born. It is what she didn't yet know that draws me to this photo. The way a moment can be captured, a moment that sits in the space between hoping and having. In this photo my mother is whole. As whole as any of us can ever be, balanced between who we are and who we will become.

I am a mother now too. I have become two women, like my mother before me. Or is it more than that? How many iterations of our selves do we carry before we lose track of our own separations? The division of before and after happens each moment, between moments, great losses happening in a silent tiptoe from there to here.

Before kids, there were grand gestures. Love came in bursts and bouquets. It came in gifts of time and trips. It was a long conversation in the dark hours of an even longer winter. After kids, everything feels long. And short too. Kids break the measuring stick. They defy metrics.

The bursts are tantrums.

The bouquets are the hyacinths from my flower garden and sprigs of mustard weed.

There is no time.

Love is a series of tiny gestures from the moment I wake up to when I accidentally fall asleep next to the smallest child.

Last day at the Freedom Farm.

• • •

I lay awake some nights, listening. It is the only quiet, and in it, I can hear myself. I can feel myself drifting back to peek once more through the hazy glass in a place gone but not gone. The Freedom Farm, with windows so old they'd begun to drip to the pressures of time, a porch roof stained with blood orange rust, losing level. Almost two hundred years, the farmhouse had pushed back Maine winters, watched spring win the battle to summer. And yet, while summer always won, the turning seasons marked fresh loss for that slanted frame. Paint cracking, floorboards bending with the cyclic shift from cold to hot and back again. Every triumphant year was also a step toward something else.

175

• • •

Flowers.

My mother planned her garden as though she was floating fifty feet above it. There were always more flowers than anything else. Some years the red, white, and blues would yield patriotic banners. Others the colors seemed to spread randomly, an impressionistic masterpiece, washed slowly away by rainstorms and wind.

On warm nights, she called quietly up the stairs, 2 a.m., 5 a.m., when the time was right to see them fall: stars—streaking through a cloudless sky—or the green shiver of aurora in the north. This is Cassiopeia and that a Dipper, she'd say, but then we'd look and look for something more. There! Tiger Lilies, orange petals waving in a summer breeze, a poppy with its petals floating up instead of down, a field of snap-dragon or was it statice, crispy in the moonless night.

All summer her knuckles were cracked, skin torn open by the dirt pressing deep into the grooves. Fingernails black, scrubbed clean, then black again. When I think of summers at the Freedom Farm, I smell freshly clipped shoots of chive growing thick in the dirt beside the house. Taste them, she'd say. We sucked and chewed, and the long blades hung from our lips as we worked. Onions, carrots, corn, potatoes, beets, and pumpkins with our names carved into their flesh. But with each ripening vegetable came two varieties of flowers, from June to September.

My second great loss is happening right now.

It is a quiet motion within my own heart—a relentless push toward a third woman I do not yet wish to meet. She knows, unequivocally, the answers to questions I have just now begun to ask.

She is a mother who will not carry another baby. Who will never again feel the warmth of five impossibly small fingers wrapping around her thumb for the first time. She is a mother moving forward, into a new space I am not quite ready to inhabit.

She is a mother who plants flowers.

I struggle to find a balance between holding tight and letting go, the place between not wanting to forget, or be too hurt by my inevitable forgetting. I struggle to stay present for joy.

Then, on a late summer afternoon, the sun hits the cheek of my little girl just so. It changes her skin to porcelain rose. Her lips become the petals of an early season iris, and her eyelashes touch her cheeks as she smiles into the warmth.

The Pond

Our home, an 1850s farmhouse, sits across the street from a beautiful and largely undeveloped pond. Someday we hope to buy the waterfront that abuts our own property, but for now, we enjoy the pond as anyone else does at the swimming hole or the town landing. Both access points are walkable and almost within sight. The whole pond stretches only a few acres from one end to the other and is home to a family of beavers, several loons, many other species of water birds, and a seemingly endless supply of fish, frogs, and leeches.

When we moved in, I hoped that the pond would be the source of many fond memories for all of us. But now, having lived here for three years, I realize it is more than that.

Bellamy loves to bring toys from her toy box to the pond. She approaches the selection with what I can only describe as frenzied indifference. Whatever toy or toys are most accessible in the moments prior to departure are the ones she'll bring. This is a child who can play for hours with any inanimate object. I was once cooking dinner and she pulled up a bench beside me and picked up a fork and a salt shaker. They began to converse about this and that, and then I heard the salt shaker whisper under her breath in an exasperated tone, "I never trusted my mother."

Bellamy was four at the time, and I hadn't realized we'd breached the topic of broken familial trust. I'd probably mentioned a handful of times that when she and her brother try to fib to me it becomes harder to trust them. But that's Bellamy for you. She takes a concept and runs with it. Though maybe that saying doesn't do her style justice. She doesn't just run with it. She disappears with it to a far-off corner of her mind. She dissects and examines new phrases, vocabulary, social dynamics, anything and everything she can get her hands on. She uses new language a hundred times over in her stories until her salt shaker can throw down an insult with the best of them.

At the pond, her toys (or sticks and pinecones if the toys lose their joie de vivre) will discuss all things nature. They notice the colors shifting in leaves as the nights grow cooler. They'll ask one another how pinecones know when to fall from trees. They join the song of the bullfrogs at water's edge with voices raised unabashedly to the skies. But this is not to say that the trivial conflicts of everyday life are off the table. There are fights over which mermaid gets to take a boat ride first and which stick has the prettiest hair. For the most part though, her personalities encourage each other to do and be more. They push one another to face fears, to swim, climb trees, even to go for kayak rides on pieces of bark.

Bellamy builds fairy houses and frog habitats and will slip into worlds that only she can reach. I often wonder if they are anything like this one, or if for her, there is a shift in texture, a slowing of time, or thickening of space that allows for the manipulation of beauty to suit her aesthetic just so. If there were a child who could design a more beautiful nature than the one that already exists, I think it would be her.

On the flip side of this delightful ability to create story from just about anything, there are times when Nathan and I get an uneasy feeling that the tether we each feel to the here and now is more stretchy and harder to grasp for Bellamy. It can be disconcerting to watch her disappear within her own thoughts. I just try to remind myself that, like all kids, it's her job to disconcert her parents. And it is our supreme pleasure to imagine what beauty and knowledge lies outside our own reach but within hers.

Our little pond fills with peepers in spring. Their shrill voices rouse us all to the shore in the still-cool April evenings. As the land around us thaws, the first signs of new life refuse to let us slip back to winter with their endless enthusiasm for the coming warmth. We sit as a family at the kitchen window in the early morning hours. The sun rises pink above the pond, and the water glimmers so bright it hurts our eyes.

The kids and I have put bird feeders in the protective branches of the lilac beside the house. Spring birds who have found the pond but not yet settled down to build their nests visit the feeder to gain strength for the coming work of raising their families. Oggie, at three years old, can identify the chickadees and goldfinches with ease. He howls with delight when a cardinal couple or a rogue cedar waxwing makes an appearance, screaming, "New birds! New birds!"

The water, still too chilly for swimming, calls to the kids the way water does. Its glassy surface ideal for skipping stones. These children will dig for the perfect flat rock in the rough sand at the water's edge, fingers pink with cold. They grasp their choice between thumb and pointer finger, cock their arms the way they've been shown a hundred times, and flick with wrist and elbow working together. Jack can get his stones to skip five or six times already and while the younger two claim to be attempting the same, it is clear they are in it for the size of the splash and not the number of times their rocks can kiss the surface before succumbing to the water's will.

Oggie cannot seem to get enough of the splashing water. He can stand by the pond's edge until his fingers are so numb they don't listen to his brain when it tells them to move. This upsets him not because of the discomfort, but because he is worried that they aren't his anymore. After all, if your body doesn't do what you tell it to, is it yours? Oggie is a complicated case. A hard nut to crack with so little time on this earth.

At three, he's very capable of expressing himself, but the way in which he does is often surprising to us all. He had trouble turning off the faucet a few days ago and came into the kitchen to inform us that the bathroom sink was out of batteries. This made perfect sense to him. When other things in his realm don't work (a remote control, an automated race track, a toy piano), it's often because of dead batteries.

Nathan and I wonder whether the number of children we now have (four) might be to blame for some of Oggie's misunderstandings. It seems that the more kids you have, the less you have time to explain the workings of the world to the younger ones. Oggie is often left to figure out the specifics of reality on his own. For better or worse, it seems that in many cases, he doesn't bother. He is comfortable residing in the space of the here and now. He is comfortable living in joy completely outside of reality's complexity. He is willing to throw stones into a pond to watch the splash until he is too cold to move. Each eruption of droplets in the brisk spring air is worth the discomfort.

Each stone thrown brings just enough joy to override the tingling in his hands until it doesn't.

He is not yet old enough for us to grasp the fullness of his personality, but we have an inkling of where it is heading. He is our first prankster. Just recently, Oggie has begun to surprise us with his jokes. His sense of timing couldn't be better. There is a sweet spot with humor. Break a joke off too soon and you don't give your audience time to buy in, make it last too long and it's not funny, just annoying. Oggie has an intuitive understanding of this balance that makes us nervous for the years to come. Just this morning he came screaming into the living room holding his head like he'd been hurt. Nathan and I jumped to action to determine the seriousness of the injury. Oggie waited until we were completely invested before stopping mid-cry to look up at us with a twinkle in his eye and a giant grin. It was shocking really, how convincing he'd been. He saw the surprise in our eyes and in return, we saw how we'd just entered into a humor arms race of sorts with our three-year-old.

When asked where he thought he was born, Oggie told Nathan it probably happened in a zoo. While technically this is completely incorrect, it is also absolutely true. This family is wild, out of control, smelly, and sanctuary to a wide variety of animals. I have no doubt that Oggie's truth will keep us all grounded someday.

• • •

Summer on the pond is always too short. By the time the water has warmed enough to swim, the kids are making two or three trips a day to cool off. They are much more willing to brave cooler waters than I am, but even so, the swimming season only lasts from late May to early September.

Our kayaks glide gently across the pond, Jack on his own and Nathan ferrying smaller kids back and forth to view the frogs and turtles who hide in the reeds along the shore.

At the far end of the pond, the land is completely wild. Over 200 acres of forest wrap around the water as if to protect it from the noise pollution of roadways and campers. With the help of kayaks, the kids are able to experience the quiet of those woods. They sit along the mossy shore with peanut butter and honey sandwiches while they listen for loon calls and feel the warmth of the sun on their skin. These are moments I want to remember. The silence— the brief seconds where these small people are growing into the gentleness of nature.

For Jack, the pond has been a conduit to independence. While his father and I both work, he walks with the smaller kids and our au pair Ally to the water. Every morning, weather permitting, the crew loads up a stroller with snacks, drinks, sunblock, and a variety of toys to drown, fight, or bury in the sandy soil by the water's edge. Bellamy and Oggie argue over rights to the better of the two stroller seats and Jack jaunts happily ahead, hands mostly free and spirits high. Each journey begins with a brief exchange in which he convinces Ally to carry his tackle box so that, according to him, he can manage his pole with an appropriate level of care. Though it should be noted he is on his third pole due to aggressive tugging, poor decision making, and general incompetence. I highly doubt he's anywhere close to reaching an appropriate level of care.

Jack is a person with unlimited energy and unyielding desire to engage anyone and everyone in a scheme. That scheme changes fairly frequently, but boy, when you're snagged by his charisma, you're walking the fine line of an event horizon. Too close and you'll never escape, too far and you'll miss the fantastic machinations of a seven-year-old brain exploding with potential. Jack is a kid who needs to struggle and fail to eventually succeed. He doesn't appreciate the easy things as much as he thinks he does.

In the spirit of cultivating a kid who approaches struggle with gusto, Nathan and I make a point to engage in experiments we are quite certain will fail. As long as they have a fun factor that speaks to our sense of the absurd, we'll go along with just about anything for a little while. One of my favorite of these experiments was Jack's two-month obsession with capturing night crawlers. These are especially long and elusive worms, ideal for catching fish in ponds that allow live bait. Jack began asking anyone who would listen for their hypotheses regarding the most effective way to catch these worms. From me, he got the simplest and most straightforward answer: dig for them. And while, like most seven-year-olds, he appreciates a good digging project, my answer didn't have any elements of danger, risk, or farm-boy ingenuity he was looking for. So, he did what most of us do when we're looking for answers that responsible people won't give us: he went to the Internet.

With Ally's help, Jack made a list of methods for coaxing worms from the dirt that did not require nearly as much effort as digging. Over the course of a few weeks, we learned some pretty foolish methods of unearthing these things.

First: grunting.

There is no level of explanation that would compare to the confusion and delight one might experience if they were to stumble upon a seven-year-old grunting for worms. To grunt for worms, one must hammer a stick into the ground. Jack tells me it is best if it's driven six to seven inches deep, but I hesitate to take him at his word. Like many firstborns, he speaks with complete confidence regardless of his actual knowledge in any given situation.

Jack spent the better part of a week hammering sticks into our yard before I noticed something was afoot. I happened to step out onto the back patio to grab my sweater from the picnic table when I spotted him with a hose, watering a rather barren spot of dirt in the upper field. My policy is typically hands off when I notice a child doing something strange, quiet, and harmless, however I do draw the line at frivolous water usage. So on this day, after about 30 seconds of observation I can't help myself. "Jack! Why are you watering the dirt?"

"You can turn it off, I'm ready to grunt." He yells this with nonchalance. He doesn't even look up to get my reaction to a new term.

"Grunt?" I yell back, staying calm and feigning only mild interest while turning off the hose at the spigot.

"Come see. The night crawlers are going to wiggle right to the surface."

Of course, I am now very interested. I've passed the point of no return in what is sure to be a cockamamie plan and there's no use in trying to hide it. As I approach, I can hear the melodic clucking of wood rubbing against wood. Jack has used his handsaw to flatten the end of the stick he hammered into the ground. (Feel free to take a moment to quietly pass judgement on the safety of allowing a seven-year-old to use a saw while I mention that we also are the type of parents who let our kids do increasingly dangerous things with sharp tools if they prove they can do them responsibly.) With another stick, he is rubbing the flat head of the stake so that it vibrates the earth beneath the surface.

"What is that supposed to be doing?" I ask, trying and failing to hide a smile.

"The vibration causes the worms to come to the surface," he explains. "They don't like it. It makes them afraid that a mole is digging toward them and they try to escape by coming up out of the dirt."

I find it extremely difficult to imagine a night crawler feeling afraid. I find it difficult to imagine a night crawler feeling much of anything. But I stand and watch Jack make those sticks hum for about fifteen minutes, while he assures me that worms will be showing up any second now.

A reasonable person might give grunting a shot once or twice before determining that it was an Internet prank. Jack on the other hand, hammered no less than fifty sticks in various locations around the property. Maybe the worms liked the soil around the compost. Maybe they didn't hang out in the shade. Maybe the ground needed to be watered so that they could slip more easily to the surface. I watched him grunt for days in every possible iteration of this activity. He never saw a single worm.

When the sting of the failed grunting wore off, Jack went back to the Internet and found an even more impressive tactic. He came into my upstairs office to pitch the idea.

"Do you have a 12 volt battery?" He wasn't going to give up the plan all in one go.

"Why?"

"I have another experiment to try."

"That's a car battery buddy. That's some serious juice."

"I know. But I'll be careful."

"You're going to jump start some night crawlers?" I had him smiling with this comment. I had myself smiling. Jack could sense my mood was good, so he went all in.

"No. But kind of? I need a battery to hook up to two metal poles that I'm going to hammer into the ground about two feet apart. When the electricity goes through the ground, the worms don't like it so they come to the surface."

On this particular day, I was in a "yes" mood. I also knew that I didn't want any part in electrocuting worms. Thankfully, I knew some-one who could almost certainly be persuaded to take part in this activity. My father.

My kids call my father "Happy" instead of Grandpa or Pops. It was a nickname that started with the first grandchild and for some reason, stuck. I looked Jack straight in the eyes and said, "I'm not zapping worms with you, but I know someone who would probably love to try something as insane as that." I kept my eyes locked on his and waited for him to come to the same conclusion I had. It didn't take long.

"Happy! He'll do it! Let's go to Gammy and Happy's house! Can we go there for dinner?" Jack was buzzing now. He started collecting all of the things he needed for an afternoon with his grandfather.

When we got to my parents' house, a short drive from our own, the smaller kids went to play in the living room while Jack ran out to the workshop to convince Happy to get a battery and some metal rods ready. Sure enough, twenty minutes later, I see the two of them in the back yard, hammering metal pins into the ground with a sledge hammer and hooking the truck battery up to them with jumper cables. They spent forty-five minutes moving the pins closer, watering the dirt, revving the engine. Nothing worked. When my dad pretended to electrocute himself and let out a blood curdling scream, we all laughed and Jack knew the experiment was over.

Autumn is my favorite season. The red maples around the pond begin their slow transformation through the color wheel of foliage demise. First, blotchy red stains appear against vibrant green.

Some leaves fall prematurely, but most hang on a little longer, fighting the cool nights and afternoon breezes. Then come the brilliant reds, oranges, yellows. Some years, if the nights dip down below freezing and don't come back, the change happens quickly. Other years, like this one, when the nights hover at the tipping point for weeks on end, the leaves do their own dance between living and dead. The color lasts and lasts until the rain or wind decide to call it for the season, tearing what foliage remains from the branches, leaving the leaves to brown in piles all over the property.

The pond, which is usually invisible through summer verdure becomes visible again in autumn. Crisp mornings keep us inside, huddled over floor vents and drinking coffee in front of the woodstove. Our trips to the water slow, but the animals that overwinter are in a frenzied last-ditch effort to collect food and fatten up. Last year we stood on the road less than fifteen feet from a chubby summer beaver taking down alders the size of my wrists in less than thirty seconds. He dragged his snacks across the road right in front of us, either not noticing or not caring that we were there.

Our regular birds hang close to the feeders in autumn and the kids watch for migratory stop-ins from the rarer species. This year, a mating pair of cardinals looks to have found us.

The pond waits in silence through August heat and January thaw. It bears witness to this growing family as it passes from one season to the next and back again. Its rhythm holds steady for us as we work to find our own.

My relationship with the pond is complicated. When Nathan and the kids walk to the swimming hole to cool off, or to the landing to throw rocks and fish, sometimes I find a reason to stay home. I don't know why this water doesn't call to me like it does to them. It used to. As a child, I too swam for hours, practiced underwater flips and twirls, held my breath until my head spun and skipped rocks. It was glorious and exhausting and never got old. I suppose that I am the one who is getting older, feeling overwhelmed by this loud world.

Right now, the pond provides respite from the noise of these beautiful, wild, carefree beings by calling them away from me. Right now, that is what I need. These sweet moments of silence allow me to keep making breakfasts, helping with homework, cleaning the house, doing the laundry, having dance parties, wrestling, reading books, and pushing these children to be exactly who they are. Without the pond, the noise of mothering would be too much. Without the pond, Jack wouldn't have learned to fish, Oggie wouldn't have strong arms and back, and

Bellamy's world would be smaller by leagues.

Maybe the gift of knowing water is how it seems to know you back.

It is impossible to say what any of us will need when these children's voices deepen, when they move forward, out into the world. But I know the pond will be here to provide it. And I hope that the sound of our joy, like the ghost of an echo will live here long after we are gone.

Winter is magical on the pond. We've been lucky two of the three winters we've been here. December brought freezing cold temperatures followed by rain and then cold again. For those who don't have experience with such things, these are the ideal conditions for smooth skating ice. Our pond turns to glass. The kids are all too small to enjoy skating, but they aren't too small to huddle within the folds of a fleece blanket, wool mittens and hats pulled over their extremities as Nathan or I tug across the pond's surface their high-sided sled.

When wearing skates, it's easy to move fast, to fling the sled from side to side, or to spin in circles with dizzying speed while the kids screech with joy and a little bit of terror. When Jack sits alone, we let the sled go, watch it spin out of control as he slides across the ice until the friction of his sled finally brings him to a stop.

In winter we can walk or skate to the beaver

lodge in the cove. Their home of sticks is piled high above the ice's surface but there are no visible entrances in which to peek. The beavers are snuggled tight beneath their roof, nibbling the bark from alder branches they've dragged down below the surface to last them through the cold months.

As parents of multiple kids, we've learned how little we really know. No two kids are the same. No two kids, even ones raised with the same two parents within a very narrow period of time, are the same. But, if you pay attention and step back to watch, kids will reveal their beautiful quirky selves and you can develop tools to help them grow.

Ezra is our youngest. He is only six months old as I write this, only just beginning to laugh and babble. I can't help but wonder if he'll like the pond as much as the others. He was the only one of them not born into water.

Nathan and I can't help speculate about how his start in this world will affect his personality. We wonder if this baby, who was whisked away by ambulance to be placed within a hypothermic capsule for three days after birth, will bear invisible scars. He doesn't like to sleep against the warm skin of my chest like the others did. Is this because he first learned to sleep with freezing cold water circulating beneath his naked body? Will there be other things that Ezra does or does not do because his parents could not give him warmth until the doctors brought him back to us?

Will Ezra be stronger or more resilient because he learned to live with discomfort in those early days? Will he hold more tightly to his family, having been taken away from them once before? Will he be afraid of the cold? These are questions that will eventually be answered, and which are also irrelevant, all things considered. Ezra will be loved no matter who he is. We will protect him fiercely while we wait for his individuality to make itself known.

No matter who he turns out to be, there is plenty of room for him in all of our hearts.

Growing up on a farm, the cyclical nature of raising crops is what marked the seasons for me. In my mind, farming connected us to the land and to each other. The beans my parents grew were the thread to our collective stories. They were the framework, the foundation to Family Neves. I worried that without beans, my own children would be somehow disconnected, unable to remember their own paths through childhood with clarity. I see now a little more clearly.

Nathan and I moved to the country to raise country kids. We moved to Maine to raise Mainers. There are many kinds of Mainers, but I like to think that what connects us to each other is our appreciation of both the beauty and hardness of Maine. Long winters and short summers, muddy spring and vibrant fall, the seasons keep us always working toward the next change. Their rhythm fills us with urgency and cultivates a mindset of movement and growth.

About the Author

Jennifer Neves is a farmer's daughter who can't quite let go of farming. She works as a technical writer while also tackling the daily chores of raising people, which have proven even more time intensive than vegetables. She is the author of *Backpack Like You Mean It* and her work has appeared in *Litro Online Magazine*, and *Literary Mama*. She lives on a farm in Palermo, Maine.

Center Point Large Print
600 Brooks Road / PO Box 1
Thorndike, ME 04986-0001 USA

(207) 568-3717

US & Canada:
1 800 929-9108
www.centerpointlargeprint.com